My Journey
My Music

Beginner Piano Lessons for Kids

Melissa Chin

Cover and interior formatting by Albatross Book Co.
albatrossbookco.com

ISBN (paperback): 979-8-9851924-9-0
ISBN (eBook): 979-8-9860659-0-8

This book is dedicated to the people who have helped me become my best self . . .

TREVOR CHIN

ZOE CHIN

TREVOR CHIN JR

LAVERNE THORPE

LORI ENDERS

MARTHA MCNEIL

VERSIE THOMPSON

LORETTA ENDERS

JOHN D. MCNEIL

About This Book

The purpose of this book is to teach children to read and play music on the piano. The layout of this book makes teaching and learning music easy through creative methods that allow children to remember new concepts. As you explore this book, you will encounter original songs and artwork that celebrate Black People who've impacted past and present-day society in America. While children are learning to play piano, they are also learning Black history.

In this book, you will also meet Zoe and TJ! Through art and song, Zoe and TJ tell a story about the many adventures of childhood. The lyrics of these songs are written to inspire and to bring joy to all who read and sing them.

Contents

A Note to Parents/ Teachers

When using "My Journey, My Music" the student takes the lead with how they progress through the lesson book. Some students may grasp a unit quicker than others, and that is okay! Do not rush through the book. The music is meant to not only teach music concepts and theory, but it was written to be enjoyed! Committing to a consistent practice routine is the key to success in learning to play the piano. The book is designed in a way that even a parent with little to no musical training can assist their child in learning. It also is designed in a user-friendly way for piano instructors.

"My Journey, My Music" is filled with exercises and activities to help reinforce musical concepts. In this book, you will see practice and review sections. These steps are important to ensure the student is understanding and retaining the new concepts. There are lyrics to assist with learning the rhythm and melody of the song. Encourage the student to sing the lyrics. Singing and playing the piano helps develop rhythm, and coordination. Most importantly, have fun. Use this time to connect with your child or student and enjoy the music!

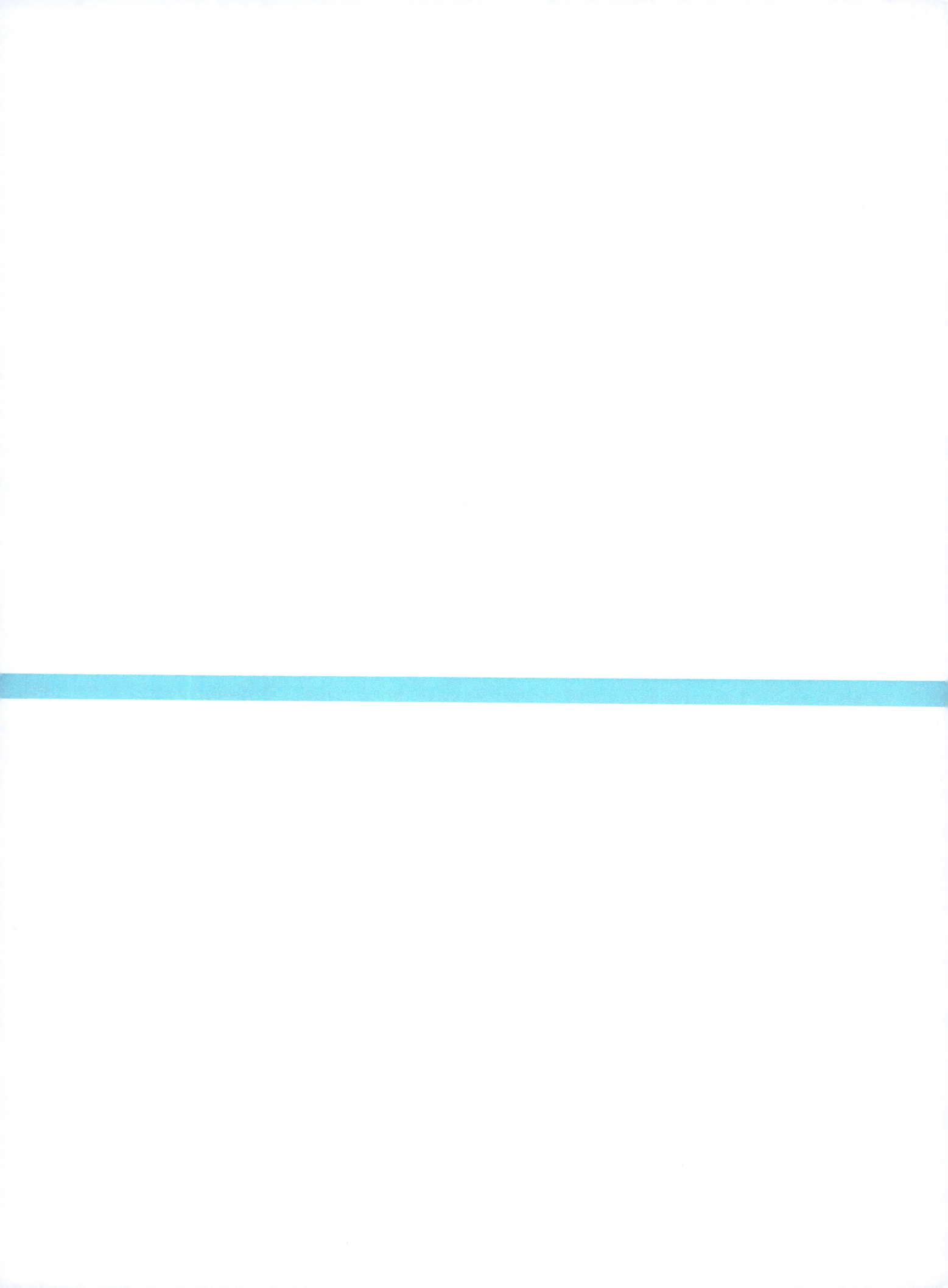

Unit 1

The Basics

The Piano

A piano makes sound when you press a key.
When you press a key, it makes a small hammer inside the
piano hit a string, which then vibrates to make a sound.
Below is a picture of a type of piano called the UPRIGHT PIANO.

ELECTRIC PIANOS and **KEYBOARDS** make sound when a hammer sends an electric signal, which then amplifies a sound through a speaker.

Take a Seat

The first step to playing well at the piano is finding the correct way to sit. Follow this checklist before playing each song in this book.

THE PIANO POSTURE CHECKLIST

+ Sit straight, tall and relaxed.

+ Sit on the front part of the bench, knees are slightly under the keyboard.

+ Piano bench (and you) should be facing the piano.

+ Sit so that your arms are on the same level as the keyboard.

+ Reach your arms straight toward the fallboard.

+ Your knuckles should just reach the fallboard. If your arms are bent, you're too close. If your knuckles don't reach the fallboard, you're too far away.

Gimme' Five

To play the piano, rest your fingertips on the keys. When you do this, it forms a natural curve. Think of a ballerina standing on her tippy toes!

In the Spotlight

Misty Copeland

Misty Copeland (1982) was born in Kansas City, Missouri. On June 30, 2015, she became the first African American woman to be promoted to principal dancer at American Ballet Theatre (ABT).

Each finger is given a number:

1,2,3,4 and 5

Practice!

+ **Trace your left and right hand**

+ **Number each finger correctly**

LEFT Hand   RIGHT Hand

Explore More!

Have a parent/teacher/friend call out various finger numbers and you wiggle those fingers

Get on Up!

Down 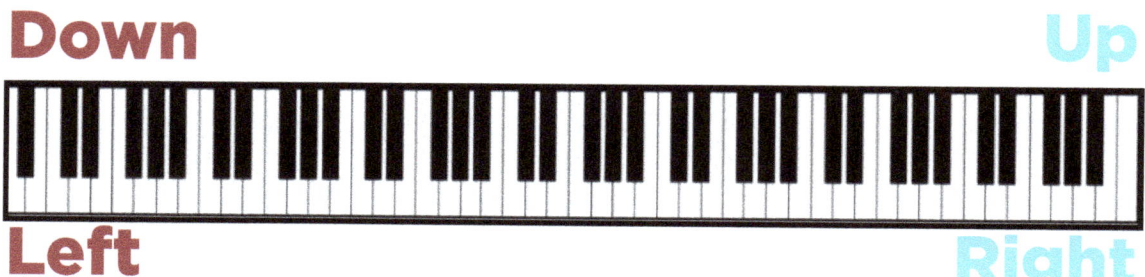 **Up**

Left **Right**

Practice

+ Use your **LEFT** hand to play some low notes

+ Use your **RIGHT** hand to play some high notes

+ What do the low notes sound like?

+ What do the high notes sound like?

 ### Get Creative!

+ Color the groups of two black keys purple
+ Color the groups of three black keys blue

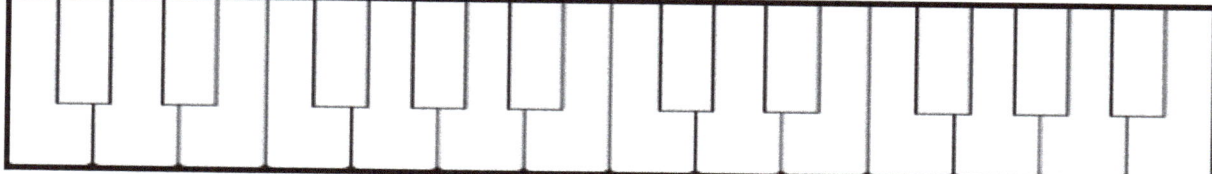

In the Spotlight

James Brown

James Brown (1933-2006) was born in Barnwell, South Carolina. He is known as the Godfather of Soul. His unique musical style of funk and soul influenced many artists. Brown used his music to inspire change, creating songs such as "America is My Home" and "Black and Proud."

Get Right or Get Left

Review Time!

+ **How do you rest your hand on the keys?**

+ **Where are the high notes? Low notes?**

Practice

+ **Color finger numbers 2 and 3 red**

Practice

+ **Find the lowest group of two black keys on your keyboard**

+ **Using your LEFT hand (LH) fingers 2 and 3, press both keys at the same time**

+ **Starting from lowest to highest, use LH fingers 2 and 3 and play all the groups of two black keys**

Get Right or Get Left

Practice

+ **Color finger numbers 2 and 3 blue**

Practice

+ **Find the highest group of two black keys on your keyboard**

+ **Using your RIGHT hand (RH) fingers 2 and 3, press both keys at the same time**

+ **Starting from highest to lowest, play all the groups of two black keys.**

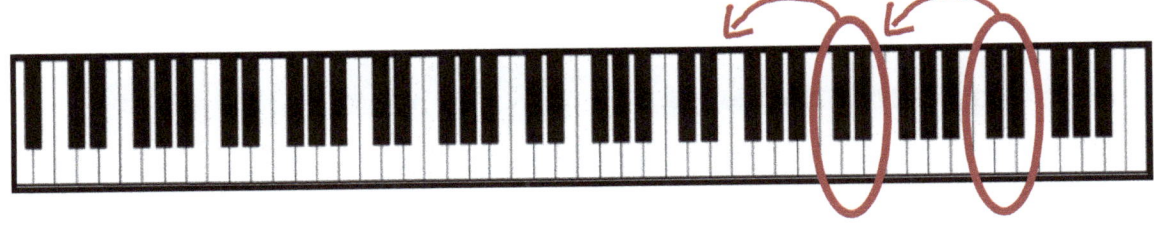

11

+ When reading music, we read left to right like a book. Keep an eye out for notes in the **RIGHT** AND **LEFT** hand.

+ The **FINGER MAP** tells you where to place your fingers for each song.

Finger Map

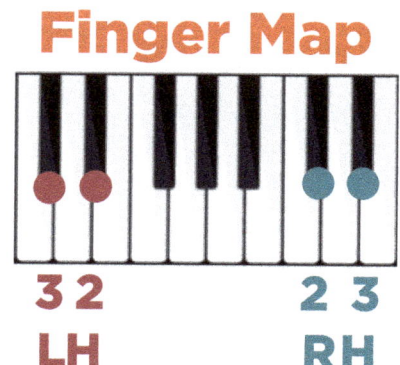

3 2
LH

2 3
RH

Practice

+ **Match your hands to the finger map**

+ **Play by pressing the finger numbers written in the song below**

Road to Success

Hint: Follow the arrows

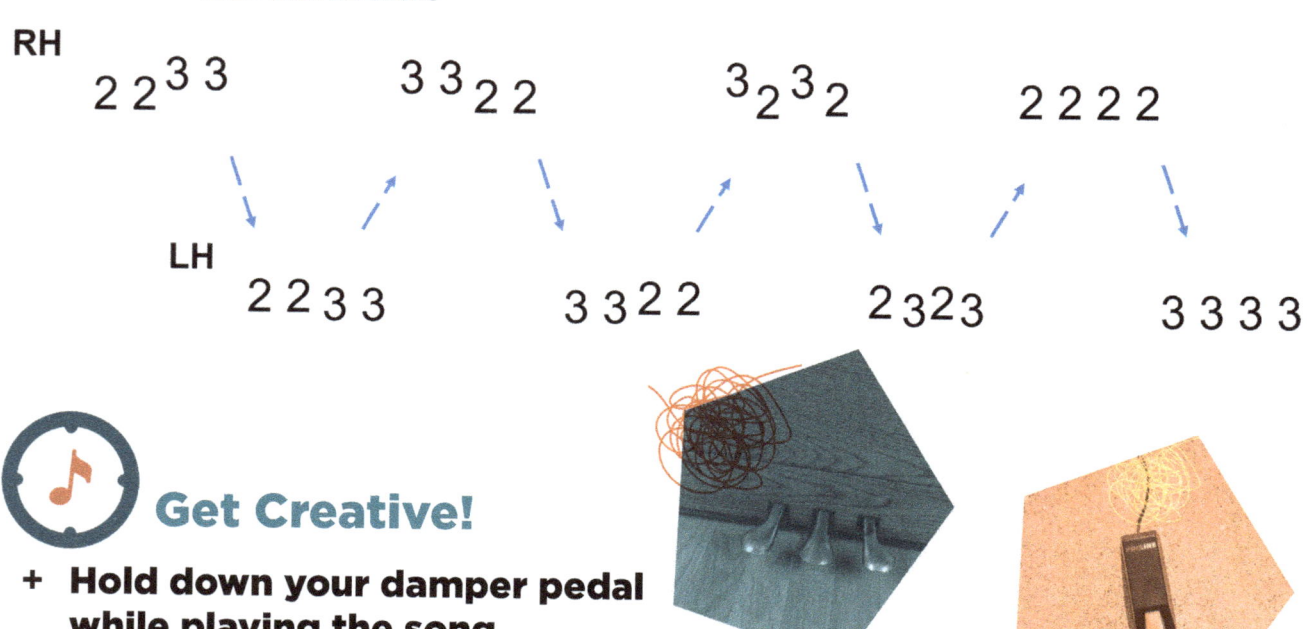

RH

2 2 3 3   3 3 2 2   3 2 3 2   2 2 2 2

LH

2 2 3 3   3 3 2 2   2 3 2 3   3 3 3 3

Get Creative!

+ Hold down your damper pedal while playing the song. How has the sound changed?

Review Time!

+ **What is the correct way to sit at the piano?**

+ **How do you rest your hands on the keyboard?**

Practice

+ Color RH fingers 2,3 and 4 purple

+ Color LH fingers 2,3 and 4 orange

+ Color the groups of three black keys black

In the Spotlight

Oprah Winfrey

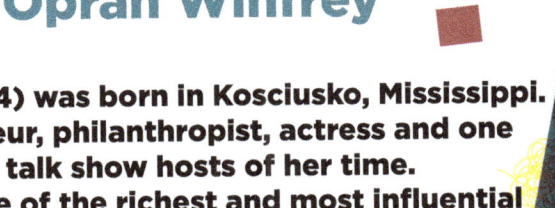

Oprah Winfrey (1954) was born in Kosciusko, Mississippi. She is an entrepreneur, philanthropist, actress and one of the most popular talk show hosts of her time. Winfrey became one of the richest and most influential women in the U.S. She used her success to sponsor many charities such as opening a school for disadvantaged girls in South Africa. Fun fact: Oprah Winfrey is left handed!!

Practice

+ **Match your hands to the finger map**

+ **Play by pressing the finger numbers written in the song below**

Finger Map

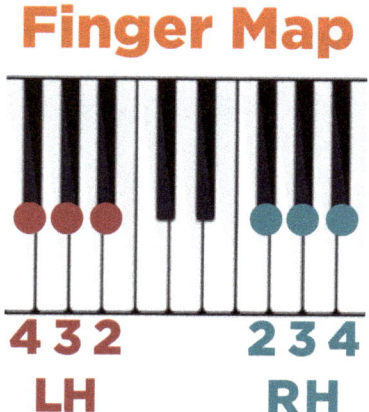

4 3 2　　2 3 4
LH　　　　RH

Three Ring Circus

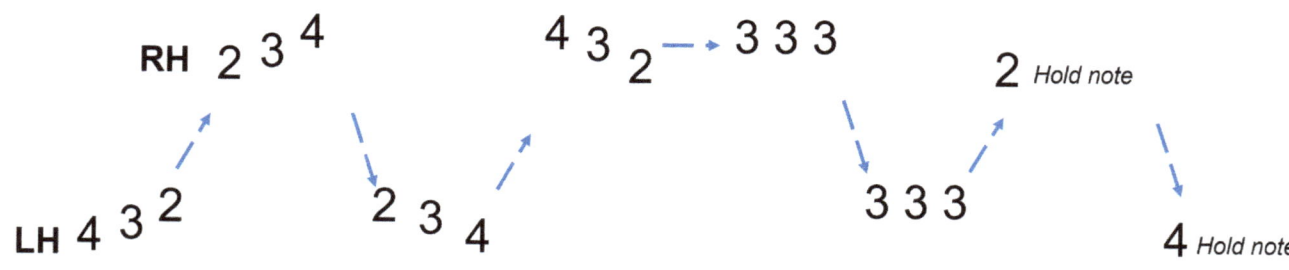

RH 2 3 4　　　4 3 2 → 3 3 3　　　2 *Hold note*

LH 4 3 2　　2 3 4　　　3 3 3　　4 *Hold note*

Unit 2

Rhythm

Quarter Notes

MUSIC NOTES tell us how long the sounds last. It tells us if it will be a short sound or a long sound.

These notes help us keep a steady **BEAT**. The beat is the same throughout the whole song.

When you clap one time for each note, that is called the **RHYTHM**. The rhythm changes throughout the song.

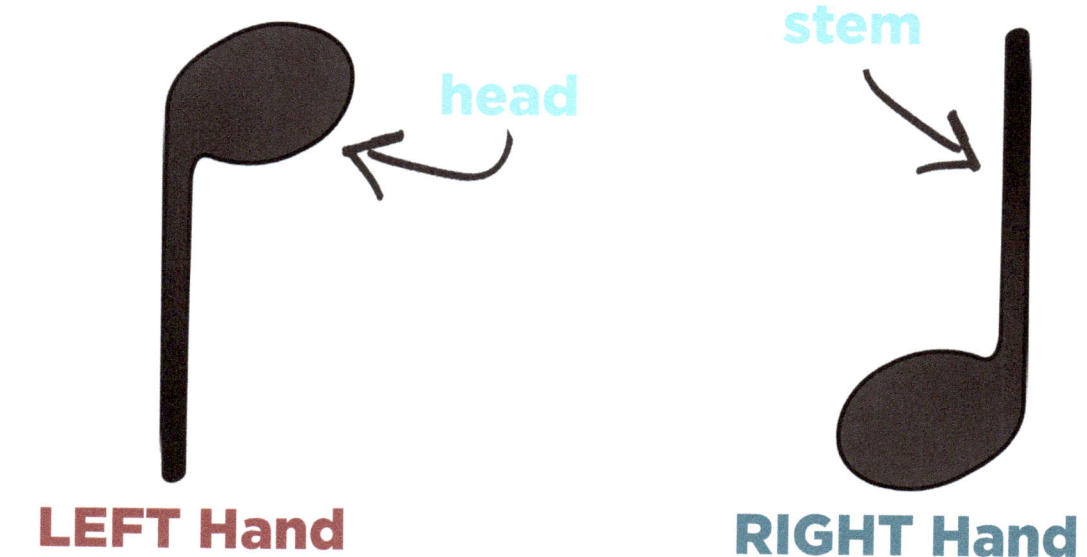

stem

head

LEFT Hand

RIGHT Hand

Practice!

+ **Practice drawing a quarter note**

Practice!

+ Practice clapping the rhythm

♩ ♩ ♩ ♩

Say: "one" "one" "one" "one"

+

Clap: 👏 👏 👏 👏

+ Practice playing quarter notes on the piano

♩ ♩ ♩ ♩

Say:

+

Play:

Practice!

+ **Clap and count the rhythm of this song**

+ **Play song while saying the finger numbers**

+ **Play song while singing the lyrics**

Finger Map

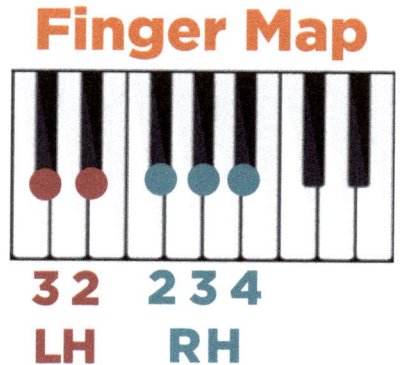

3 2   2 3 4
LH   RH

Short and Sweet

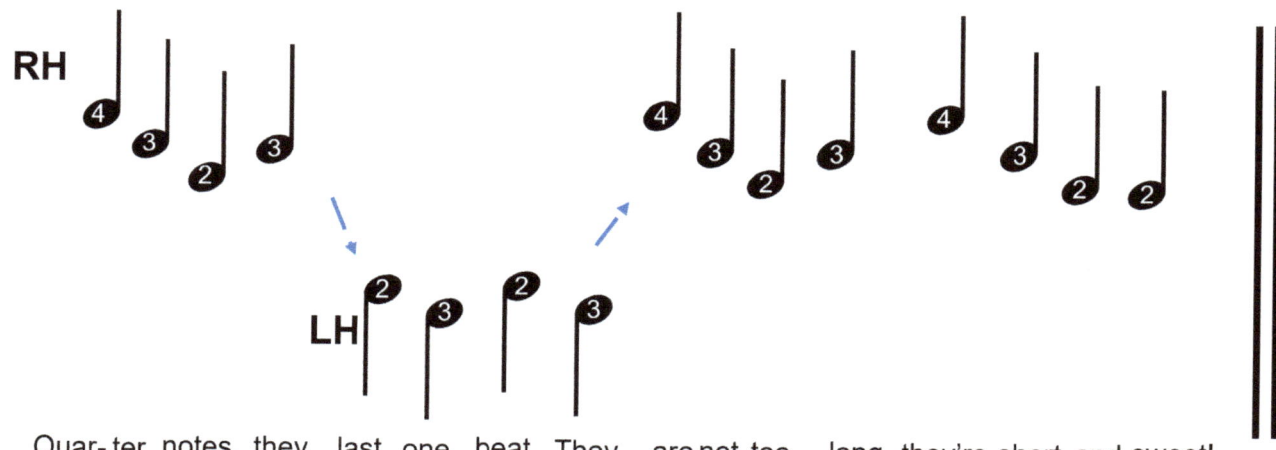

Quar-ter notes, they last one beat. They are not too long they're short and sweet!

A **DOUBLE BAR LINE** means you have reached the end of the song.

Practice!

+ Clap and count the rhythm of this song
+ Play song while saying the finger numbers
+ Play song while singing the lyrics

Finger Map

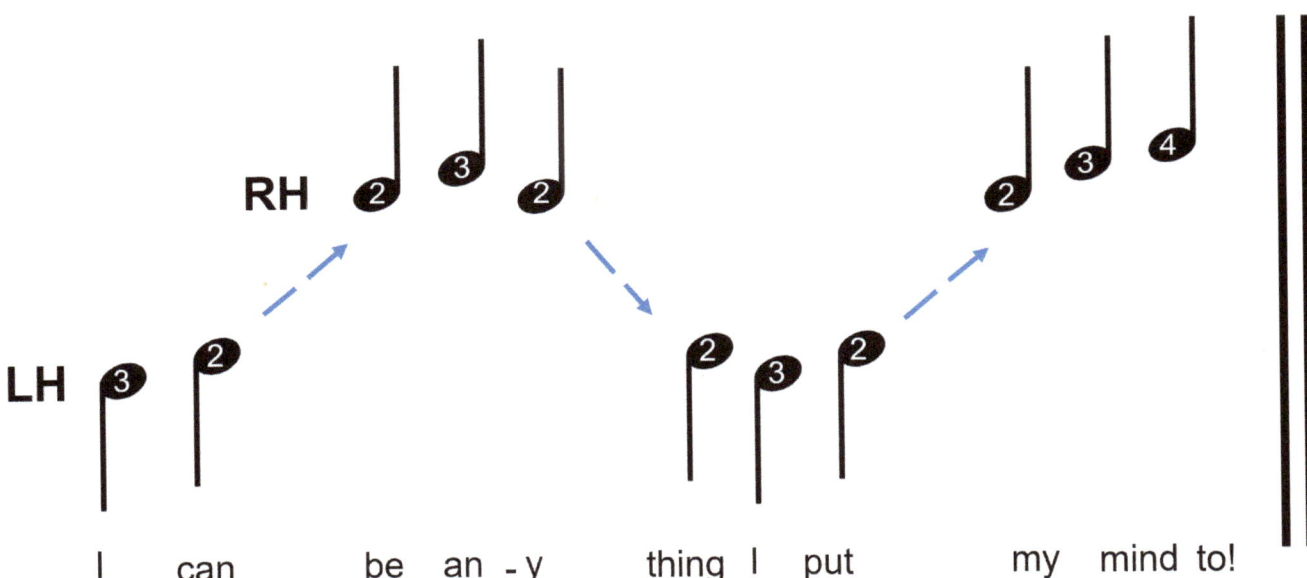

3 2
LH

2 3 4
RH

I Can Be Anything

RH ② ③ ②   ② ③ ②   ② ③ ④

LH ③ ②

I   can   be an - y   thing I put   my mind to!

In the Spotlight

Mae Jemison

Mae Jemison (1956) was born in Decatur, Alabama. She is a physician and the first African American astronaut. She flew into space aboard The Endeavor doing experiments on motion sickness and weightlessness.

Practice!

+ **Clap and count the rhythm of this song**

+ **Play song while saying the finger numbers**

+ **Play song while singing the lyrics**

Finger Map

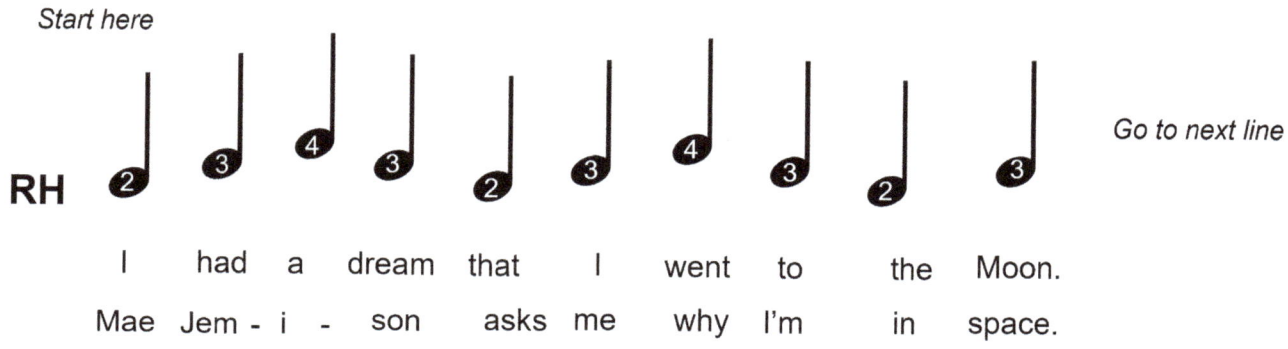

4 3 2
LH

2 3 4
RH

Trip to the Moon

Start here

Go to next line

RH

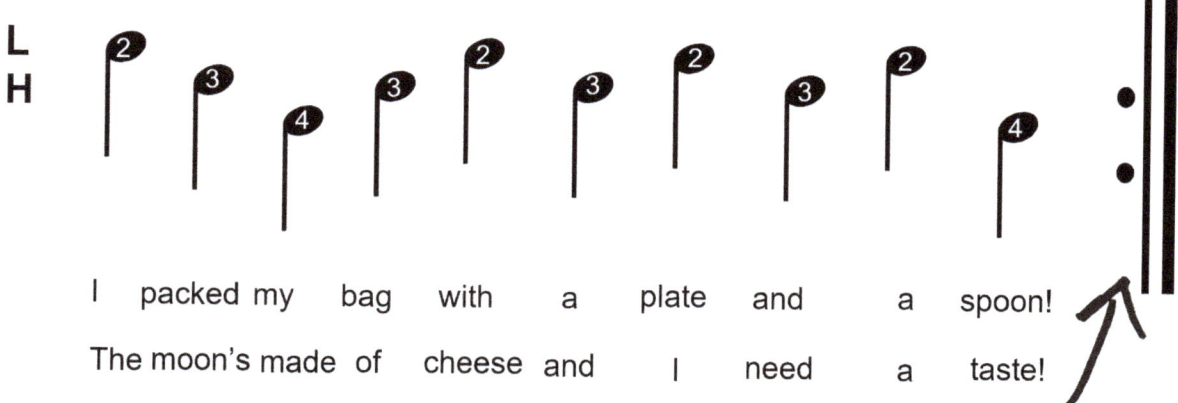

I had a dream that I went to the Moon.
Mae Jem - i - son asks me why I'm in space.

L
H

I packed my bag with a plate and a spoon!
The moon's made of cheese and I need a taste!

The **REPEAT SIGN** means to play the song again from the beginning. This song has two verses, so you will have to play it two times.

Get Creative!

+ **Can you memorize the words to the song? Play and sing along with a steady beat!**

Half Notes

A **HALF NOTE** lasts for 2 beats.

That means you will hold down a piano key and count to two.

See that a half note is not colored in.

LEFT Hand

RIGHT Hand

Practice!

+ Practice drawing a half note

 # Practice!

+ **Practice clapping the rhythm**

Say: "one, two"   "one, two"   "one, two"   "one, two"
\+
Clap:

+ **Practice playing half notes on the piano**
+ *Hint: Only press a key one time for each half note*

Say: "one, two"   "one, two"   "one, two"   "one, two"
\+
Play:

DYNAMICS are how loud or soft you play parts of a song. It can also tell you the feeling of a song!

FORTE (*f*) means to play loudly.

To play loudly press the keys firmly with your fingertips.

PIANO (*p*) means to play softly.

To play softly, keep your fingertips close to the keys and press the keys gently.

Practice

+ **Practice drawing a forte symbol**   + **Practice drawing a piano symbol**

FORTE (*f*) means to

play _____.

PIANO (*p*) means to

play _____.

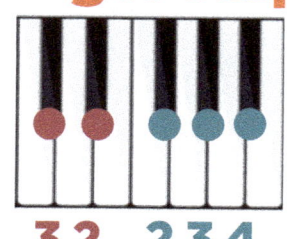

Practice!

+ **Clap and count the rhythm of this song**

+ **Play song while saying the finger numbers**

+ **Play song while singing the lyrics**

Finger Map

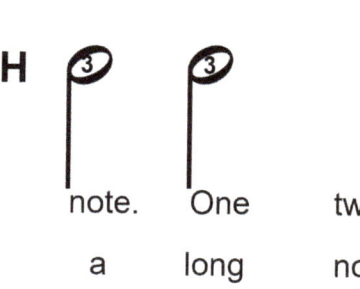

3 2   2 3 4
LH   RH

A Half Note

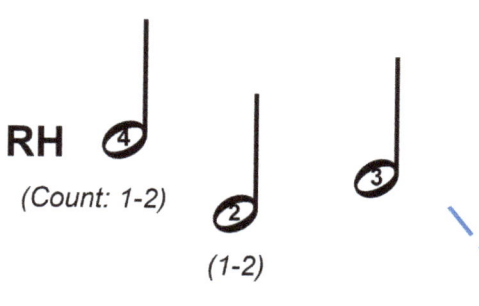

RH

(Count: 1-2)

(1-2)

𝒑 *Piano: play song softly*

LH

| Here's | a | half | note. | One | two | half | note! |
| Half | note | is | a | long | note | to | play. |

Get Creative!
Try playing the song with different combinations of piano and forte

+ What does forte (*f*) mean?

+ What does piano (*p*) mean?

Practice!

+ **Clap and count the rhythm of this song**

+ **Play song while saying the finger numbers**

+ **Play song while singing the lyrics**

Finger Map

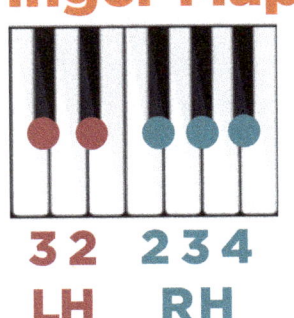

3 2 2 3 4

LH RH

Brave and Strong

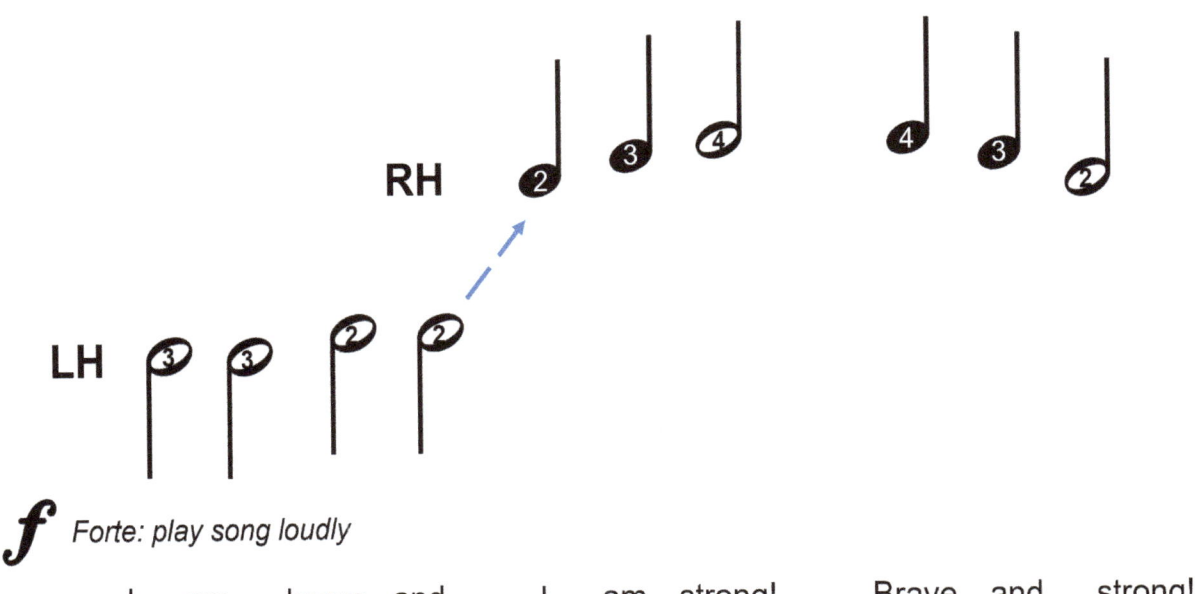

f *Forte: play song loudly*

I   am   brave   and   I   am   strong!   Brave   and   strong!

I   play   and   sing   all   day   long!   All   day   long!

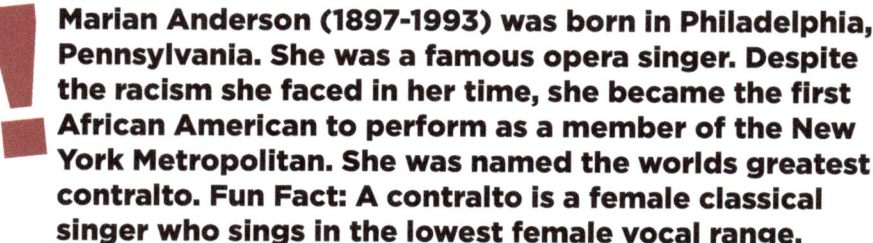

In the Spotlight — Marian Anderson

Marian Anderson (1897-1993) was born in Philadelphia, Pennsylvania. She was a famous opera singer. Despite the racism she faced in her time, she became the first African American to perform as a member of the New York Metropolitan. She was named the worlds greatest contralto. Fun Fact: A contralto is a female classical singer who sings in the lowest female vocal range.

Finger Map

4 3 2
LH

2 3 4
RH

Marian Sings For Us

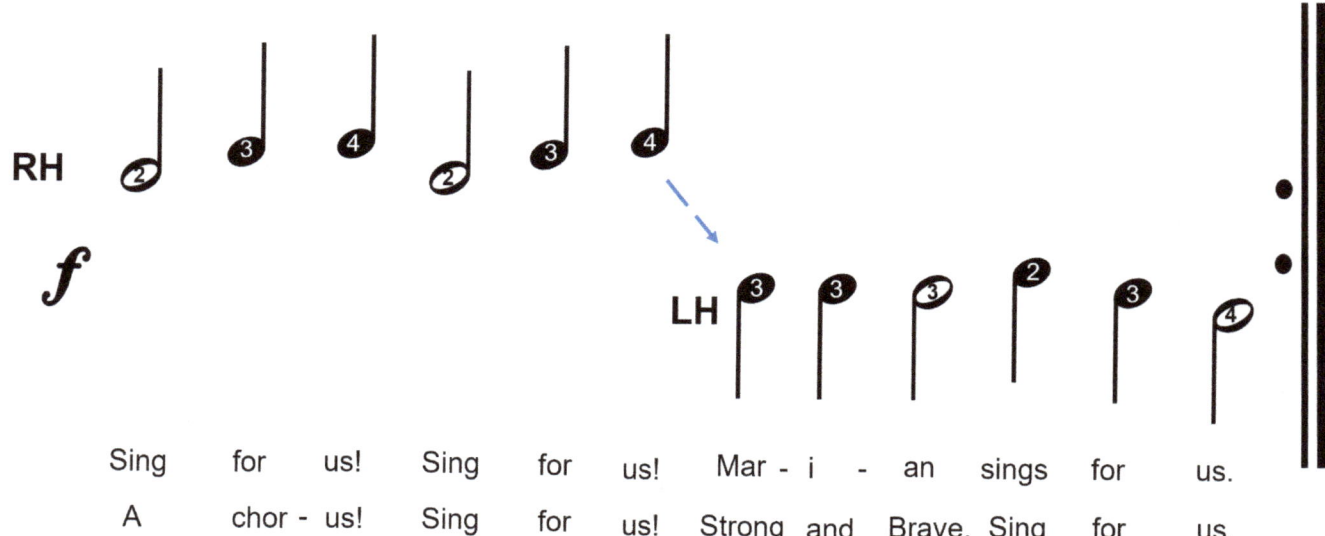

RH   2   3   4   2   3   4

𝆑

LH   3   3   3   2   3   4

| Sing | for | us! | Sing | for | us! | Mar - i - an | sings | for | us. |
| A | chor - us! | Sing | for | us! | Strong | and | Brave. Sing | for | us. |

26

Whole Notes

A **WHOLE NOTE** lasts for 4 beats. That means you will hold down a piano key and count to four.

A whole note is longer than a quarter note and a half note.

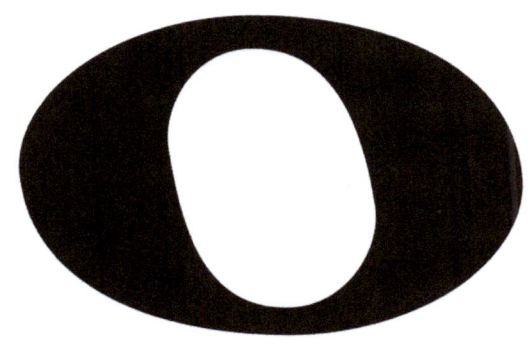

Practice!

+ Practice drawing a whole note

 ## Practice!

+ Practice clapping the rhythm

Say: "one, two, three, four"   "one, two, three, four"

+

Clap:

Say: "one, two, three, four"   "one, two, three, four"

+

Play: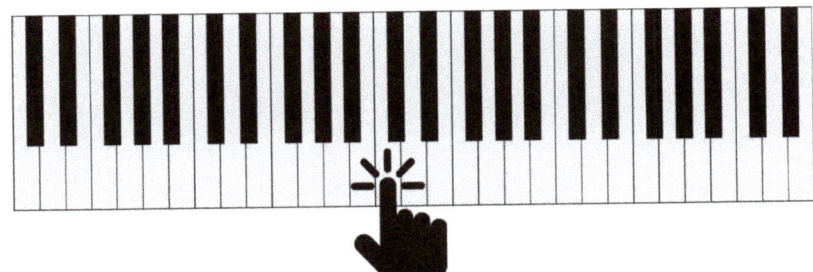

27

Practice!

+ **Clap and count the rhythm of this song**

+ **Play song while saying the finger numbers**

+ **Play song while singing the lyrics**

Finger Map

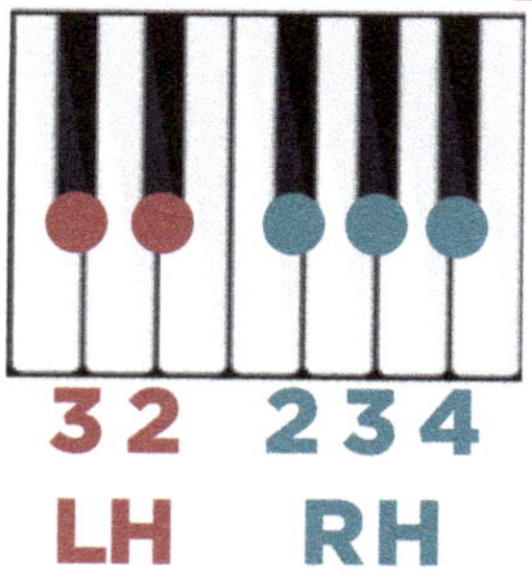

3 2   2 3 4
LH   RH

My Whole Note

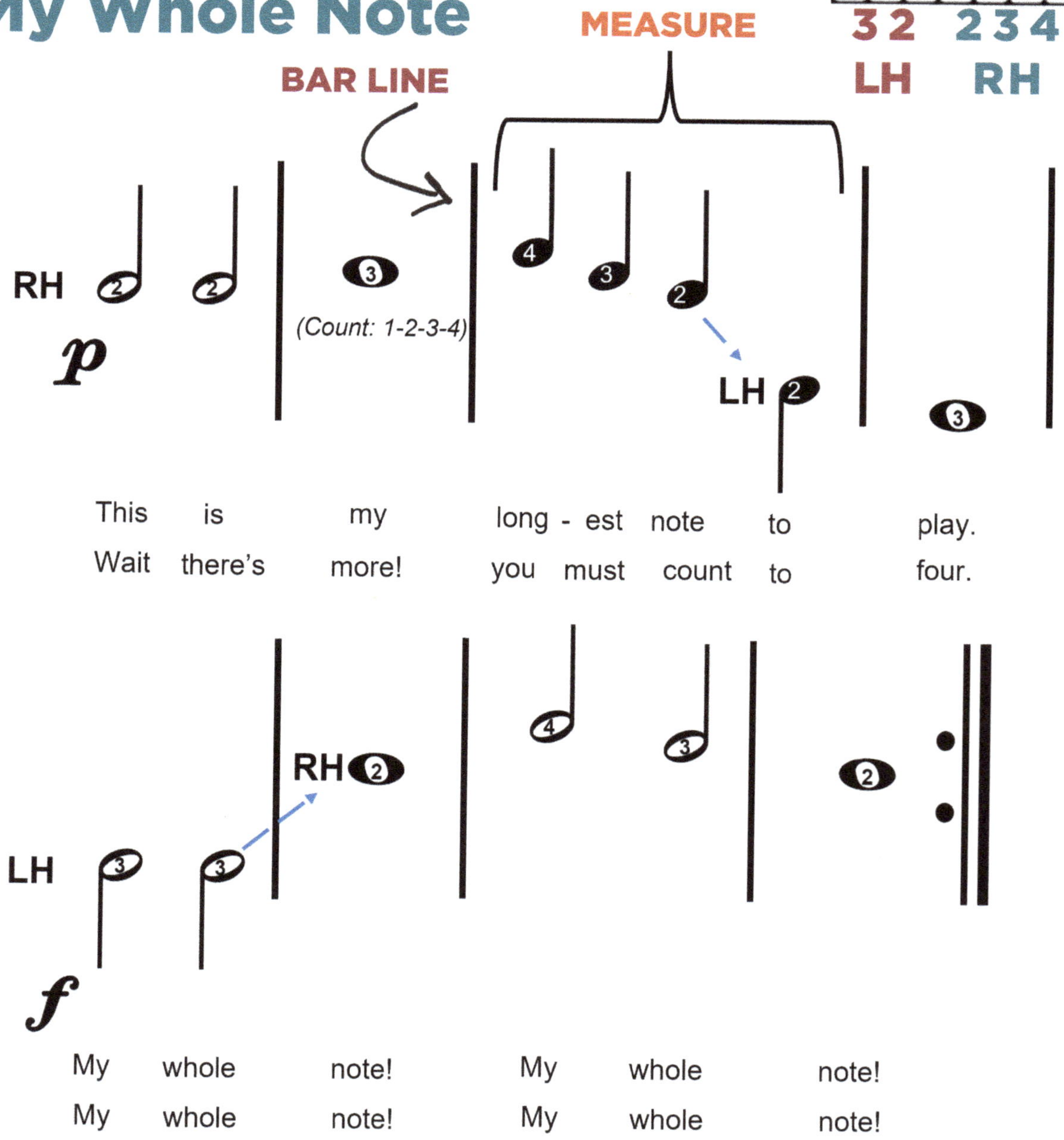

MEASURE

BAR LINE

RH ② ②

p

(Count: 1-2-3-4)

④ ③ ②

LH ②

③

| This | is | my | long - est | note | to | play. |
| Wait | there's | more! | you | must | count | to | four. |

RH ②

LH ③ ③

f

④ ③

②

| My | whole | note! | My | whole | note! |
| My | whole | note! | My | whole | note! |

28

A **BAR LINE** separates notes into equal groups. These groups are called measures. In this song, each **MEASURE** has four beats.

Finger Map

Harriet Leads the Way

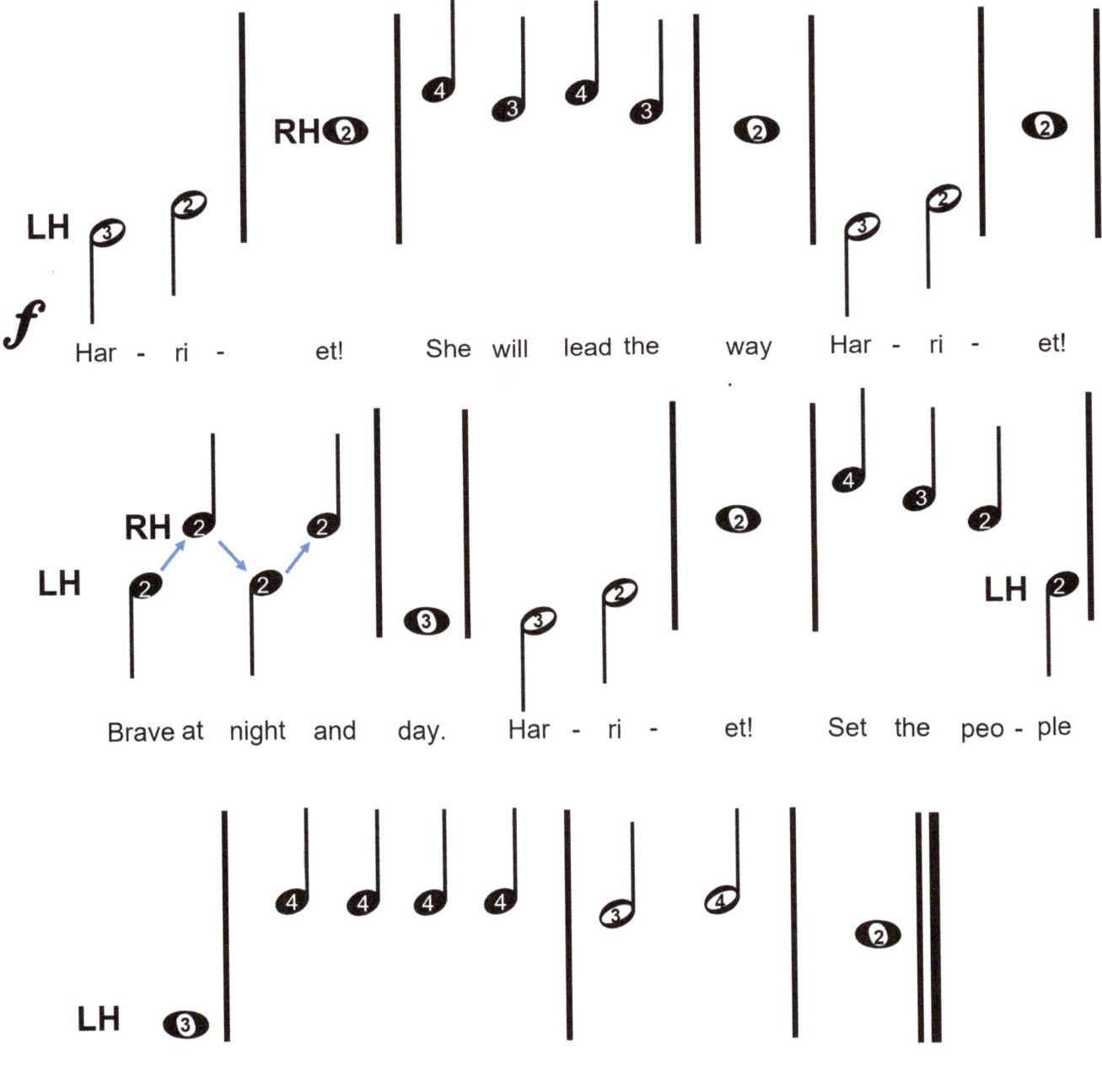

Har - ri - et!   She will   lead the   way   Har - ri - et!

Brave at   night   and   day.   Har - ri - et!   Set   the   peo - ple

free.   Changed the   world   for   you   and   me!

29

In the Spotlight Harriet Tubman

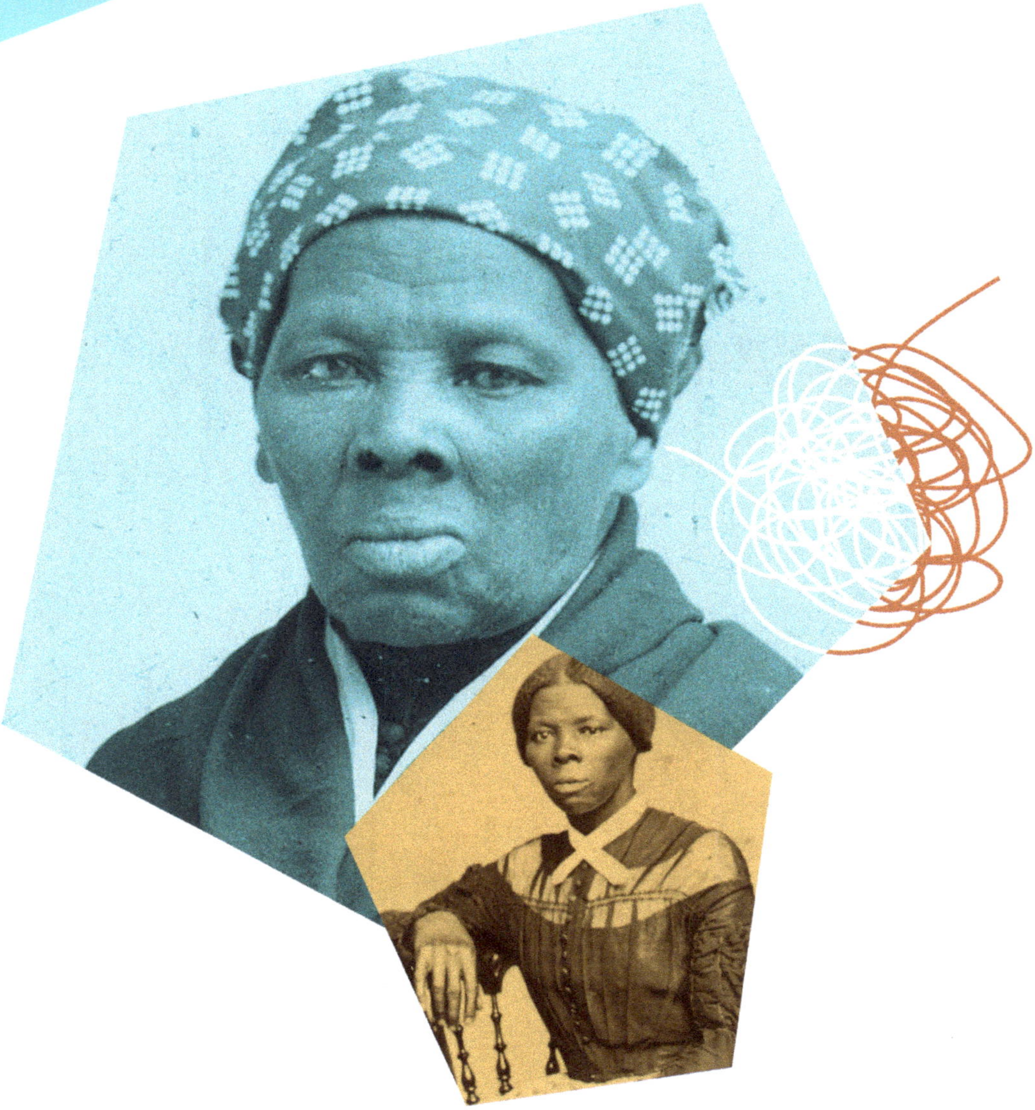

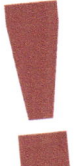

! Harriet Tubman (1820-1913) was born into slavery in Dorchester County, Maryland. She escaped to freedom in The North in 1849 and became one of the most famous abolitionists. She risked her life, leading hundreds of enslaved people to freedom along the route of The Underground Railroad.

Unit 3

Musical Alphabet

Musical Alphabet

Every key on the piano is named after a letter in the alphabet.

We only use 7 letters: A, B, C, D, E, F, and G. When we get to G, we start all over again with A.

On pianos and full-sized keyboards there are 88 KEYS. The first note is A. The last letter is C.

A B C D E F G A B C D E F G A B C D E F G A B C D E F G A B C D E F G A B C D E F G A B C D E F G A B C

Practice!

+ Fill in the missing letters of the music alphabet.

1. A,B, ____ ,D,E, ____ ,G,A, ____ ,C,D, ____ ,F,G, ____ ,B,C

2. C,D, ____ ,F, ____ ,A,B,C

3. G,A, ____ ,C, ____ ,E, ____ , ____

4. G,F, ____ ,D, ____ ,B, ____ ,G

5. C,B, ____ ,G, ____ ,E, ____ ,C

Review Time!

+ How many letters are in the music alphabet?

+ How many beats does a whole note get?

Practice!

+ Circle the CDE groups on the keyboard below

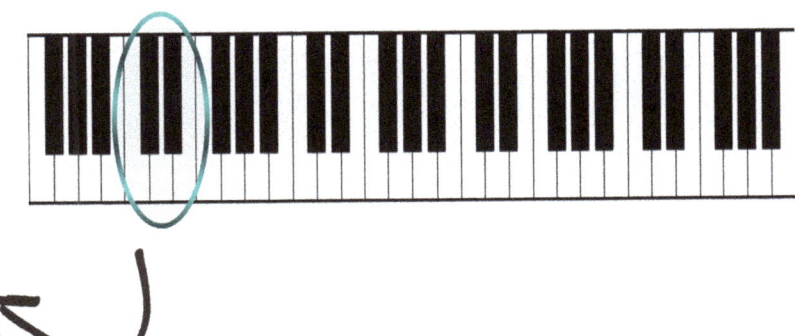

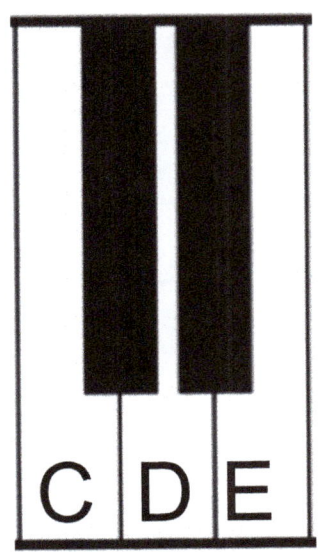

Practice!

+ Fill in the correct letters of the musical alphabet

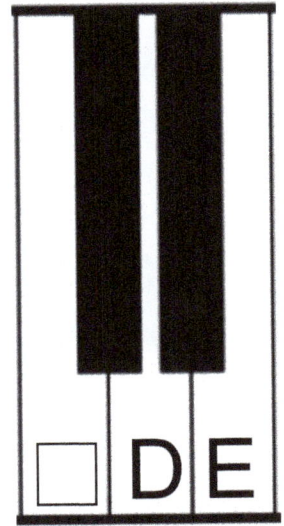 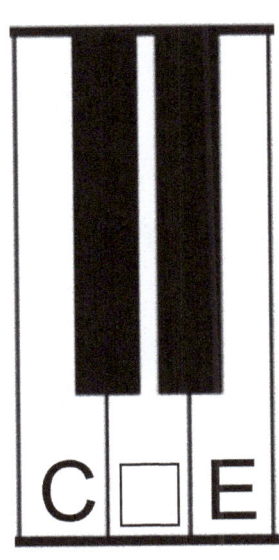 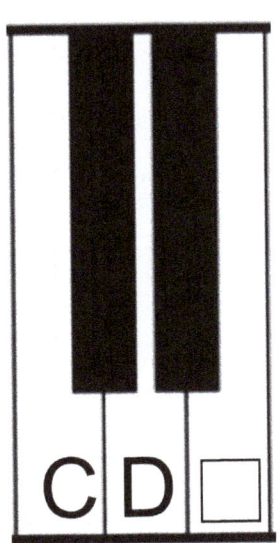 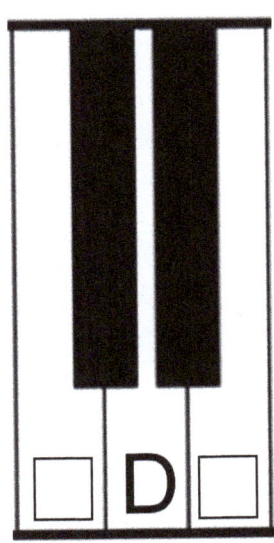

+ **Find C, D, and E on the piano**

Practice!

+ **Clap and count the rhythm of this song**
+ **Play song while saying the letters**

Finger Map

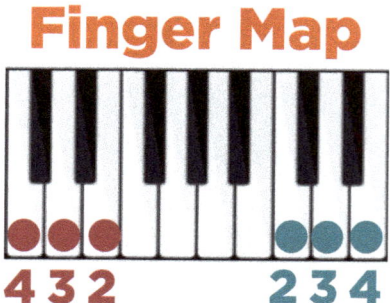

4 3 2   2 3 4

C-D-E Step

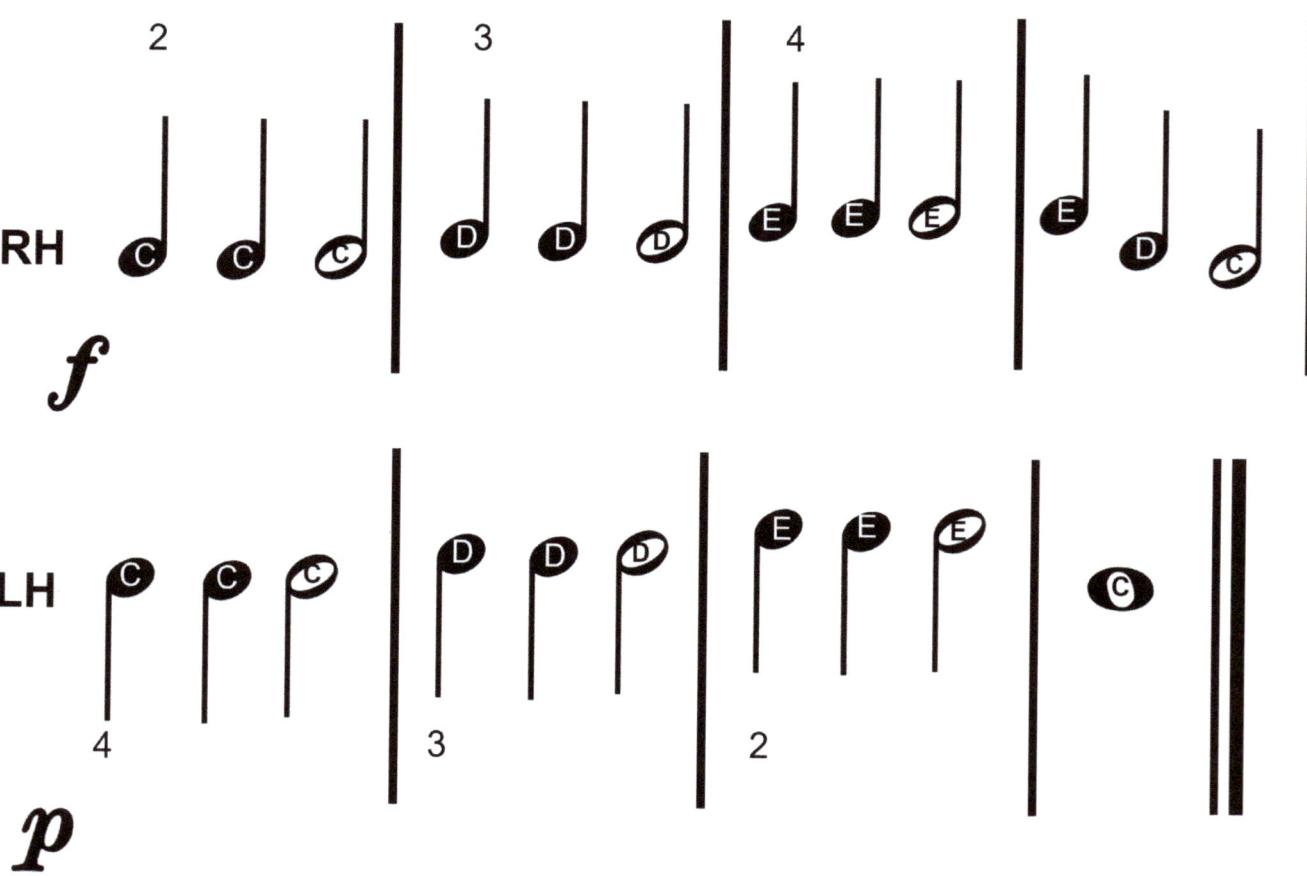

Practice!

Finger Map

+ **Clap and count the rhythm of this song**
+ **Play song while saying the letters**
+ **Play song while singing the lyrics**

4 3 2   2 3 4

Zoe Had a Teddy Bear

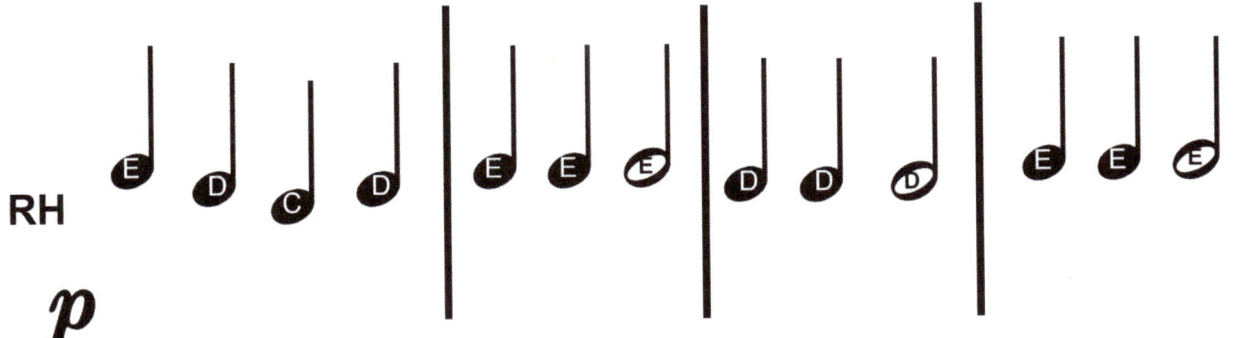

RH

p

Zo - e had a ted - dy bear, ted - dy bear, ted - dy bear!

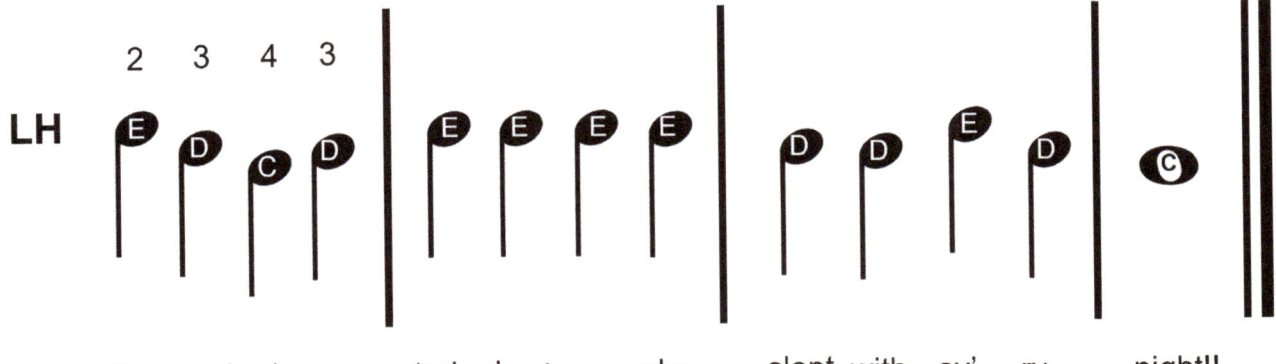

LH

Zo - e had a ted -dy bear she slept with ev' - ry night!!

MEZZO FORTE (*mf*) means to play moderately loudly; play louder than piano (*p*) and softer than forte (*f*)

Practice!

+ Clap and count the rhythm of this song

+ Play song while saying the finger numbers

+ Play song while singing the lyrics

Finger Map

4 3 2   2 3 4

Dear John

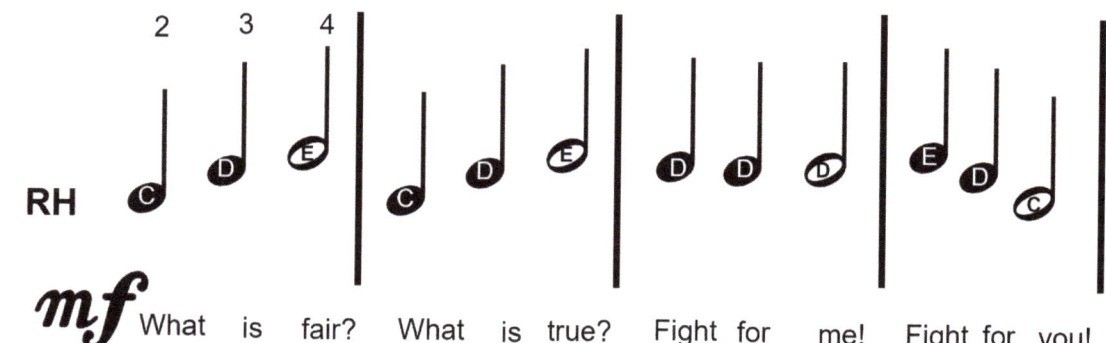

mf

Mezzo forte: play song moderately loud

What is fair? What is true? Fight for me! Fight for you!

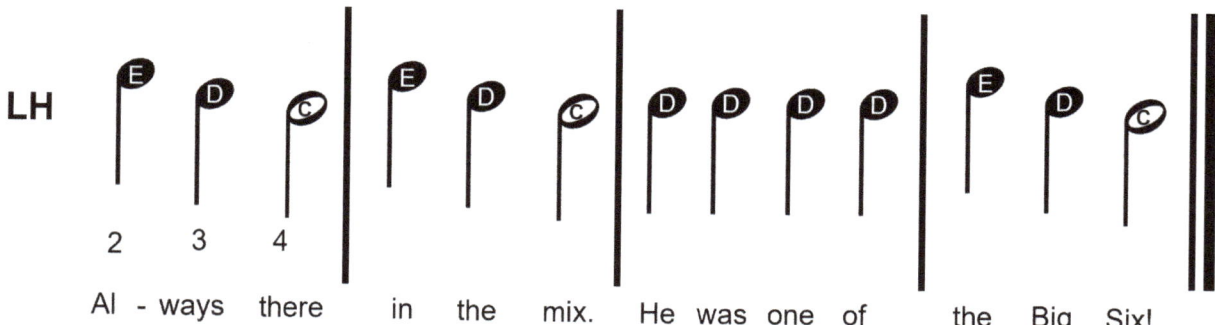

Al - ways there in the mix. He was one of the Big Six!

John Lewis

John Lewis (1940-2020) was born near Troy, Alabama. He was an African American civil rights leader and politician who served in the U.S. Congress for over 30 years. Lewis is recognized as one of the Big Six leaders of the Civil Rights Movement. As a civil rights leader, Lewis organized sit-ins at lunch counters and other segregated places to peacefully protest segregation and racism. In his early 20s, Lewis helped organize and spoke at The March on Washington.

F, G, A, and **B** are the four WHITE keys below the three BLACK keys.

Practice!

+ **Circle the FGAB groups on the keyboard below**

Practice!

+ **Fill in the correct letters of the musical alphabet**

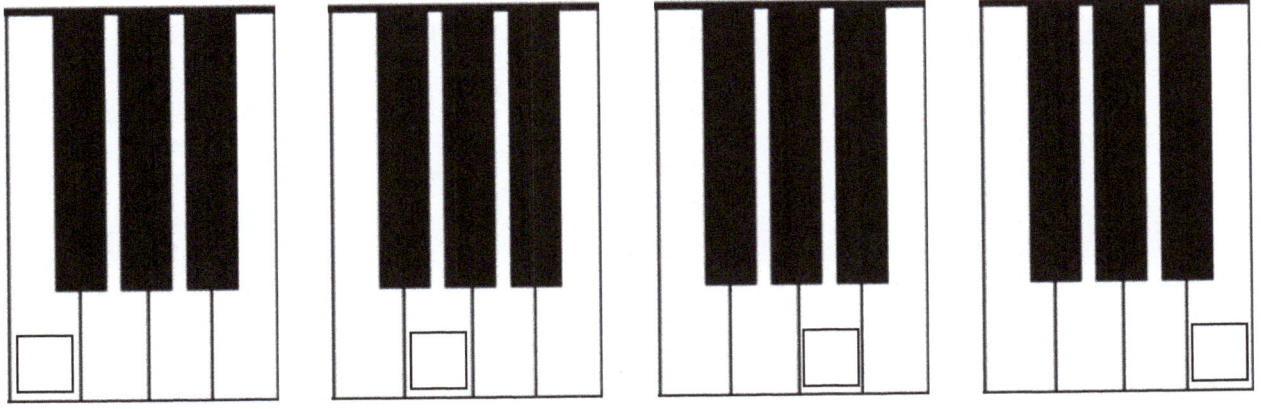

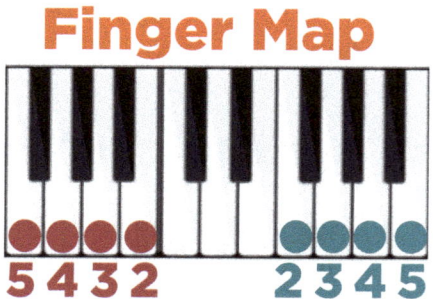

+ **Find C,D, and E on the piano**

+ **Find F,G,A and B on the piano**

+ **What is *mf*?**

Practice!

+ **Match your hands to the finger map**

+ **Clap and count the rhythm of this song**

+ **Play the song while saying the letters**

Finger Map

5 4 3 2   2 3 4 5

Floating

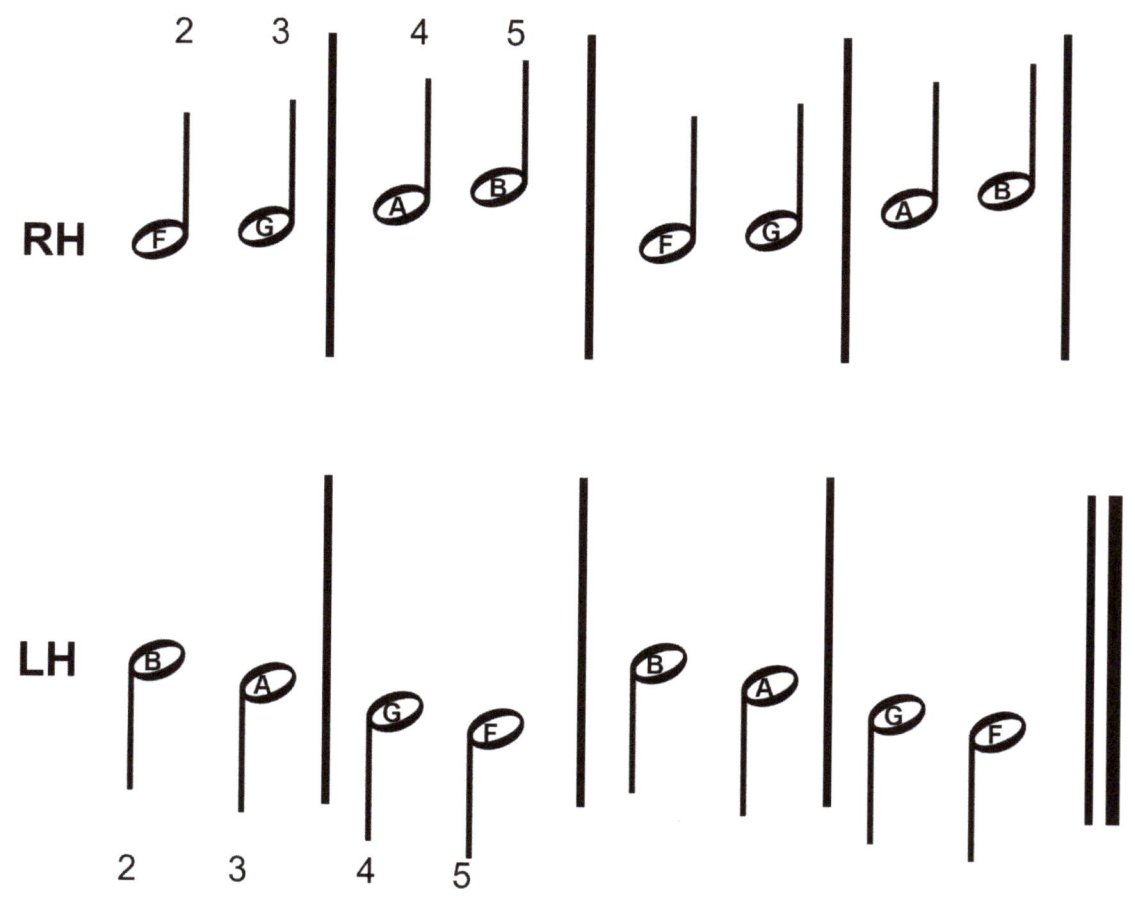

A **BASS CLEF** sign represents low notes. Play these notes with your left hand.

A **TREBLE CLEF** represents high notes. Play these notes with your right hand.

Practice!

+ **Match your hands to the finger map**

+ **Clap and count the rhythm of this song**

+ **Play the song while saying the letters**

Finger Map

3 2 1 1 2 3 4

The Park

C is the white key to the LEFT of the two black keys

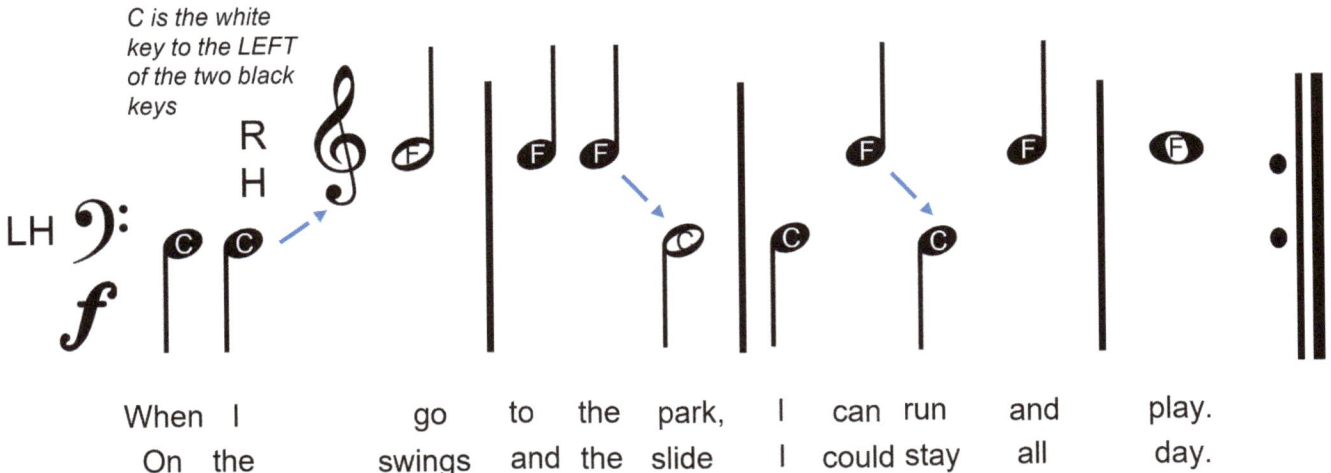

When I   go   to   the   park,   I   can   run   and   play.
On   the   swings   and   the   slide   I   could   stay   all   day.

Practice!

+ **Match your hands to the finger map**

+ **Clap and count the rhythm of the songs**

+ **Play the song while saying the letters**

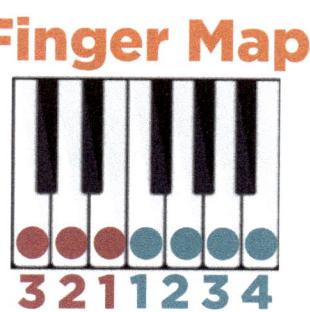

3 2 1 1 2 3 4

Thank You

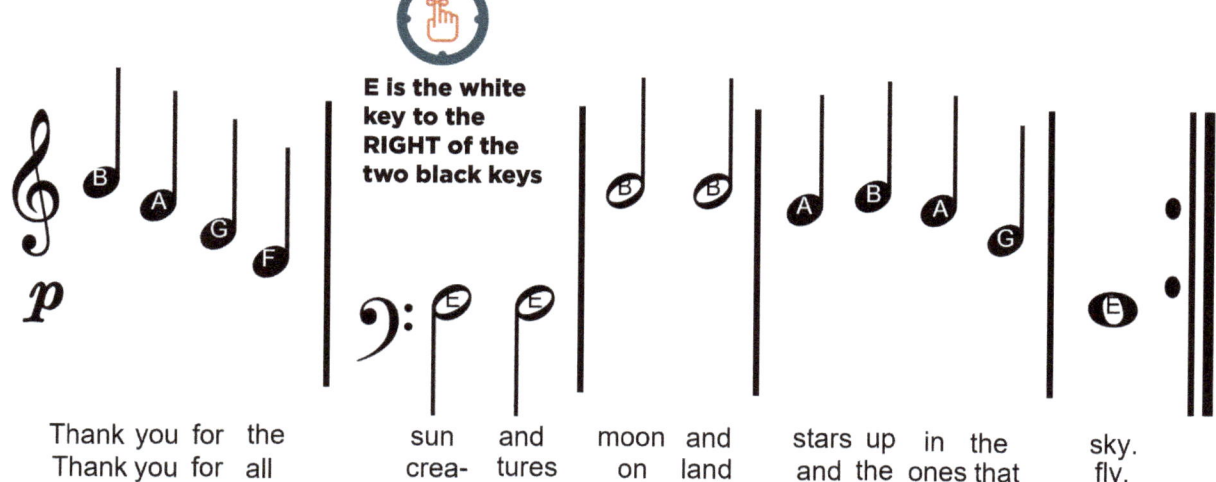

E is the white key to the RIGHT of the two black keys

Thank you for the   sun and   moon and   stars up in the   sky.
Thank you for all   crea- tures   on land   and the ones that   fly.

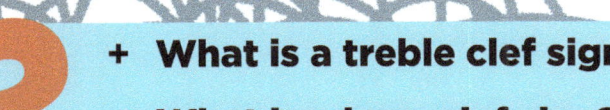

?

+ **What is a treble clef sign?**

+ **What is a bass clef sign?**

+ **Where is your left hand? Right hand?**

Finger Map

3 2 1 1 2 3 4

Let's Celebrate!

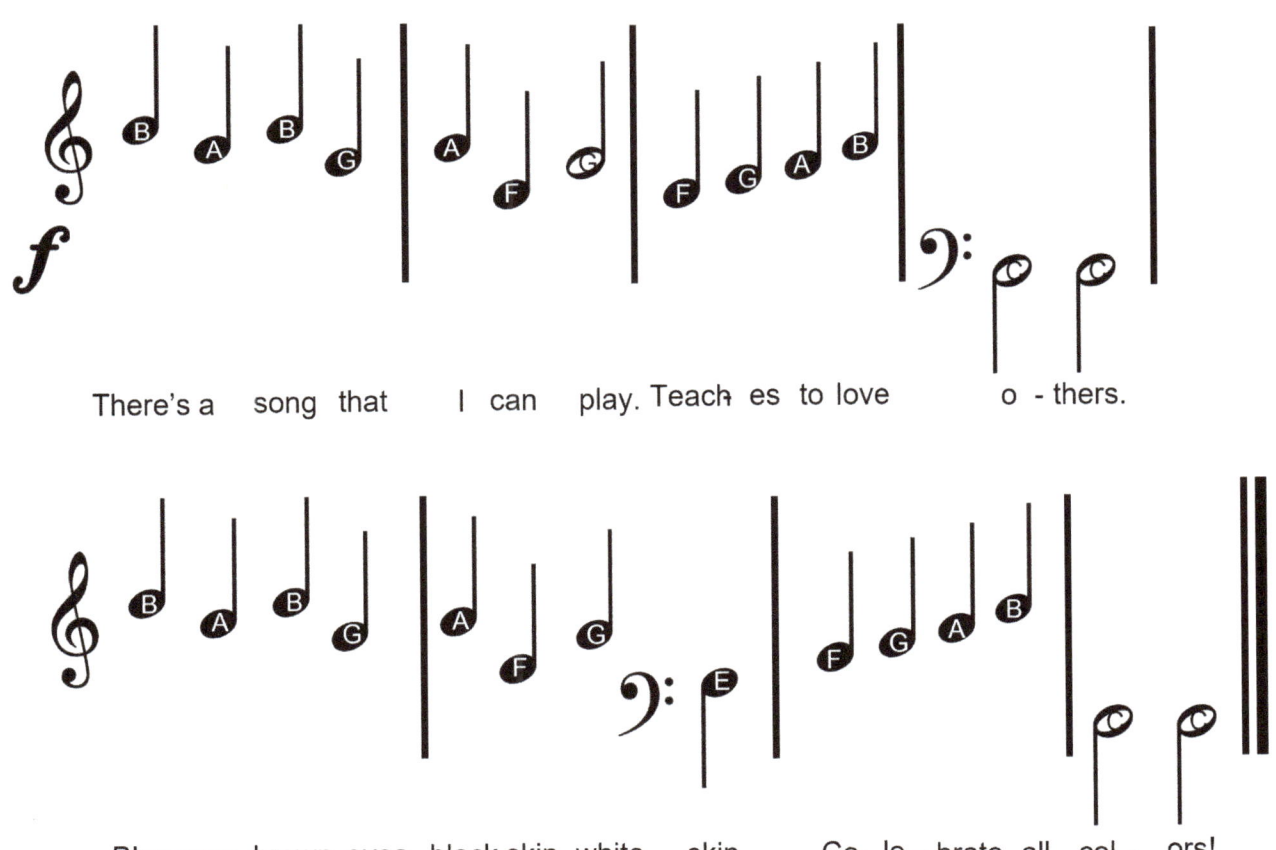

There's a   song that   I can   play. Teach es to love   o - thers.

Blue eyes, brown eyes, black skin, white   skin.   Ce- le - brate all col - ors!

41

The Freedom Singers

The Freedom Singers (1962-1966) were a musical group from Albany, NY. These four young African Americans performed songs throughout The United States to raise money and awareness for the Student Nonviolent Coordinating Committee (SNCC) during the Civil Rights Era. A popular song they performed was a well-known freedom song "Aint Gonna' Let Nobody Turn Me 'Round."

Ain't Gonna Let Nobody Turn Me Around

Negro Spiritual
Adapted

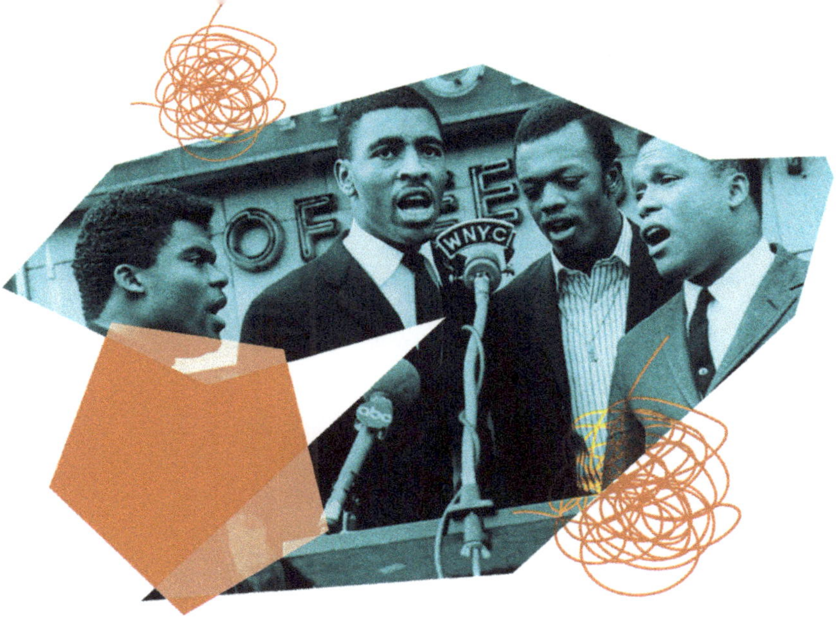

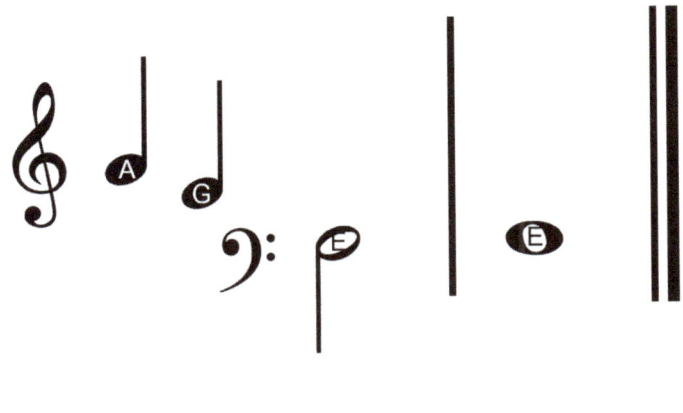

no bod - y turn me a - round I'm gon - na keep on

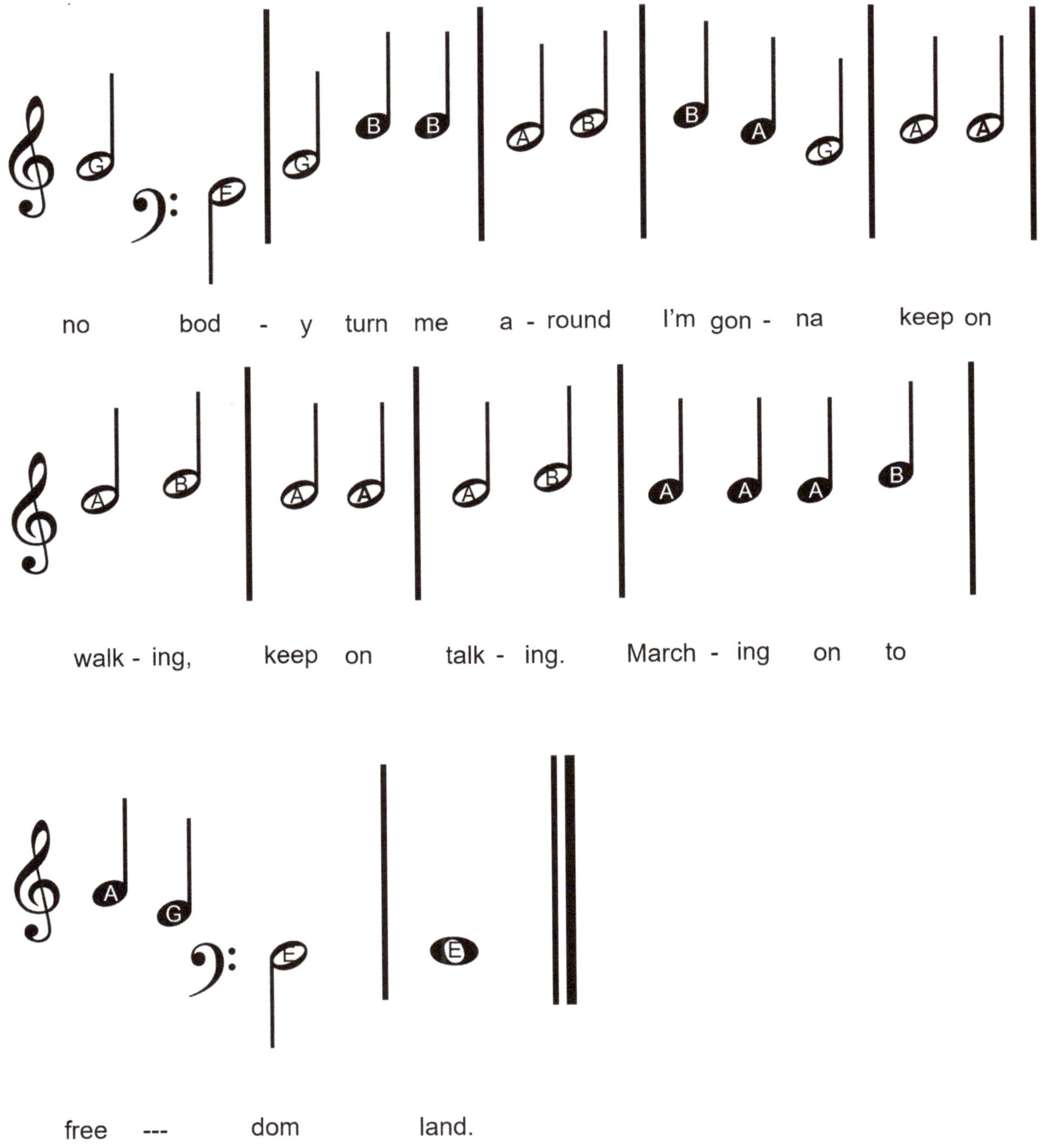

walk - ing, keep on talk - ing. March - ing on to

free --- dom land.

43

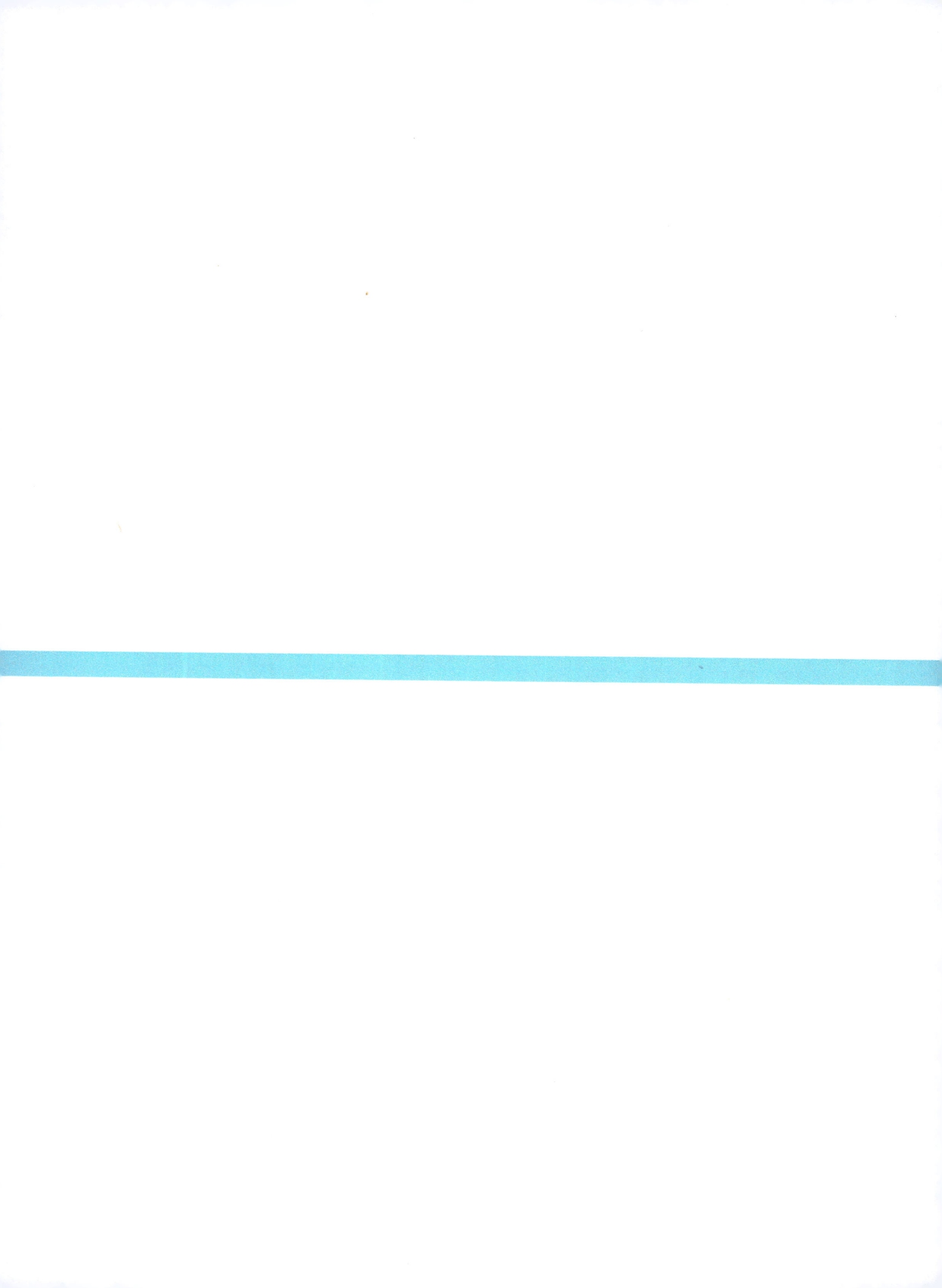

Unit 4

Music Staff

A MUSIC STAFF has five lines and four spaces. Each line and space represents a key on your piano or keyboard.

+ **Count the lines**

+ **Count the spaces**

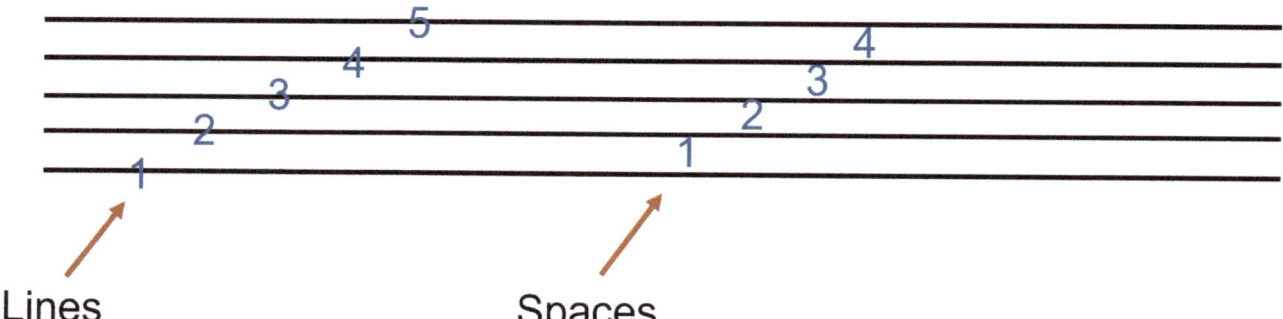

Lines   Spaces

On the music staff, there are LINE NOTES and SPACE NOTES. A line note has a line going through the note. A space note is in between 2 lines.

+ **Color in the line notes orange**

+ **Color in the space notes blue**

A music staff is like a ladder. The notes can go up and down. As the notes go up, the sounds from your piano become higher. As the notes go down, the sounds become lower.

+ **Color the notes going higher purple**

+ **Color the notes going lower black**

The Grand Staff

The **TREBLE CLEF STAFF** shows you the notes that are played with your right hand.

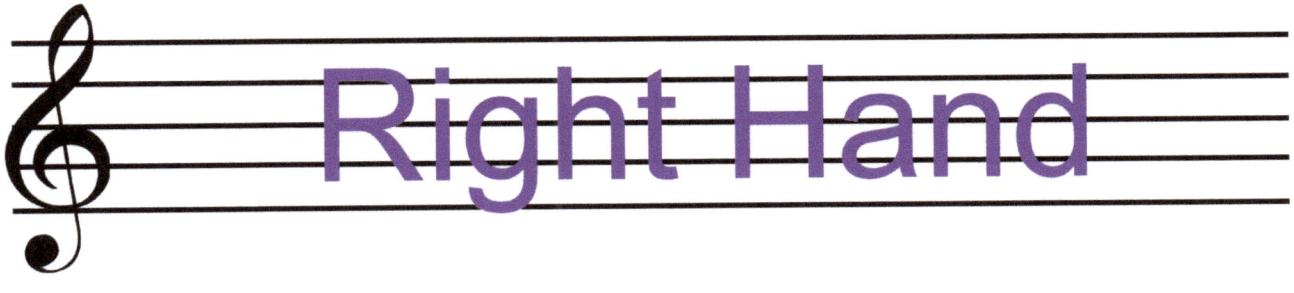

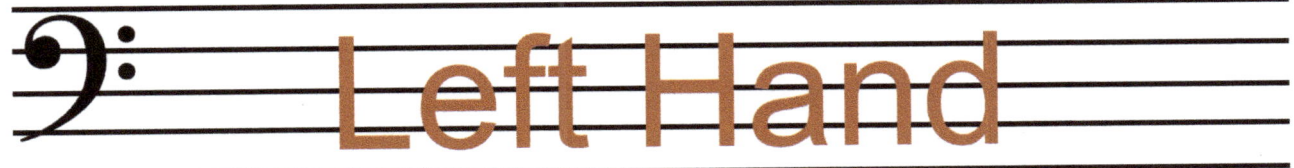

The **BASS CLEF STAFF** shows you the notes that are played with your left hand.

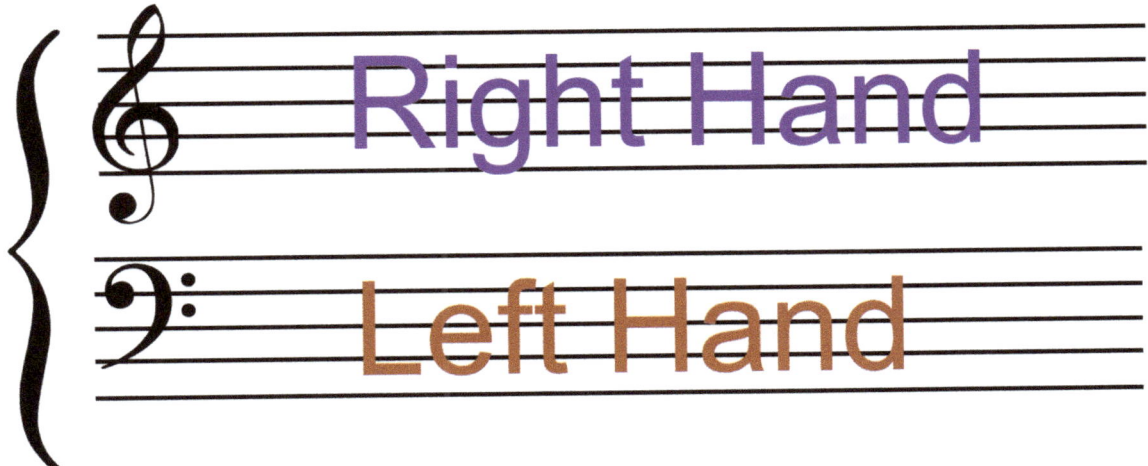

When the treble clef and bass clef are joined together, it is called the grand staff. The grand staff allows you to read and play notes for both left and right hand at the same time.

The **BRACE** connects the treble clef and the bass clef together

The Grand Staff and Musical Alphabet

The musical alphabet can be written on the grand staff more than once.

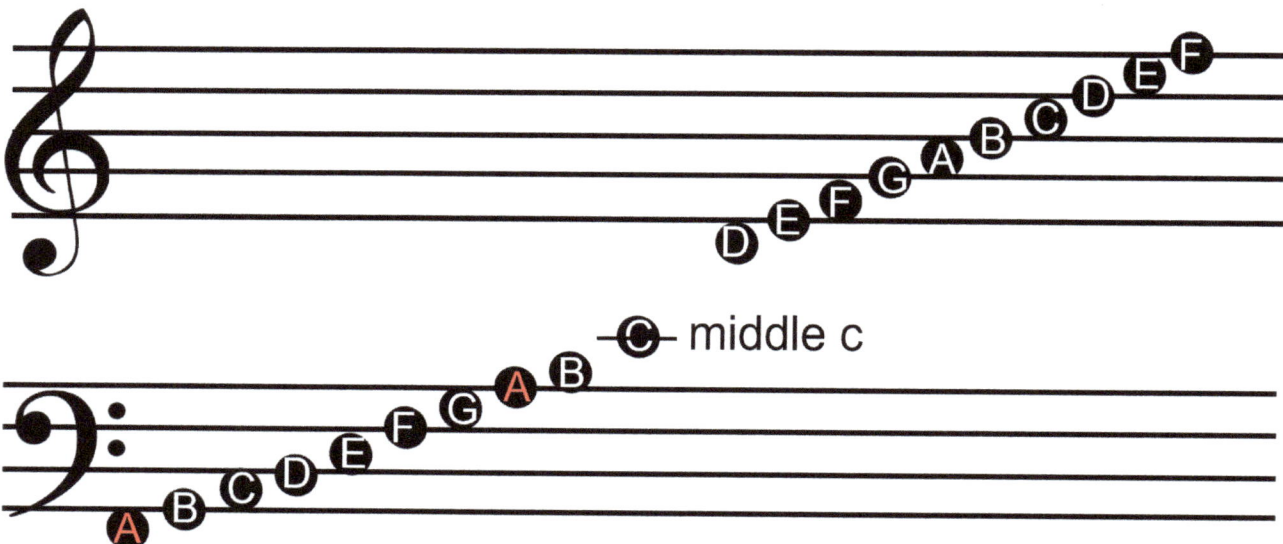

How many times can the musical alphabet be written on the grand staff?

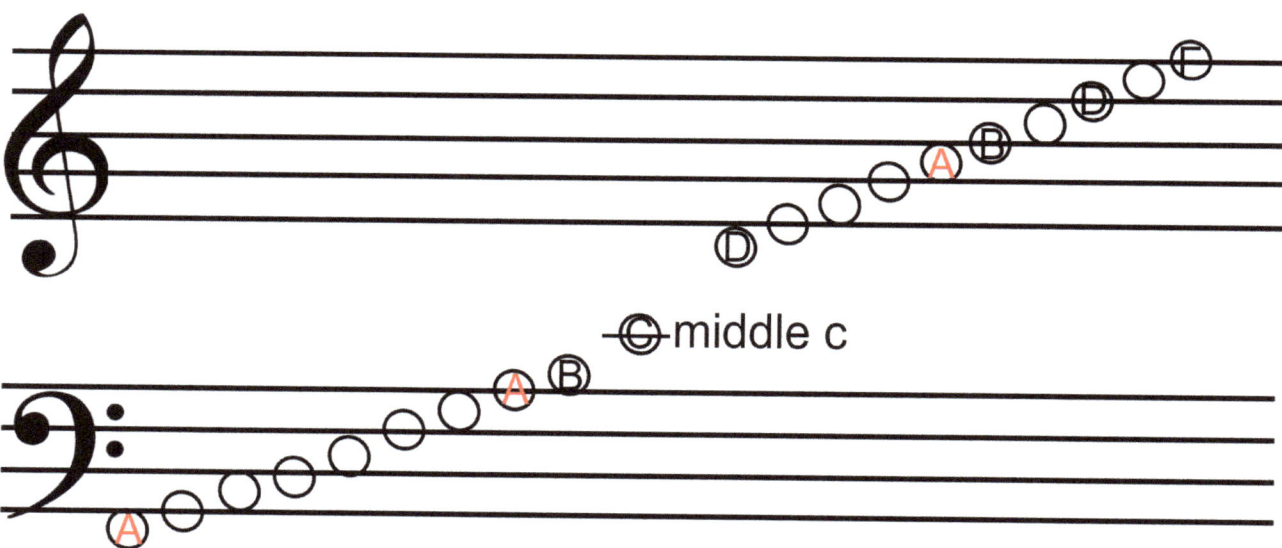

Practice!

+ **Fill in the missing letters of the musical alphabet on the grand staff above.**

Middle C

On your piano or keyboard, there are several C's. **MIDDLE C** will be the C that's closest to you when you sit right in the middle of your piano or keyboard.

On a piano or a full-sized keyboard, middle C is the 4th C starting from the left.

Practice!

+ **Find middle C and color it in (hint: middle C is the 4th C from the left)**

+ **Find middle C on your piano or keyboard**

Middle C is written on a short line called a **LEDGER LINE**. It is placed between the two staffs.

Practice!   + **Draw middle C**

+ **Play the middle Cs below**

+ **Find middle C**

+ **With what hand do you play notes on the treble clef? Bass clef?**

Review Time!

MIDDLE C is closer to the treble clef when you are to use your right hand.

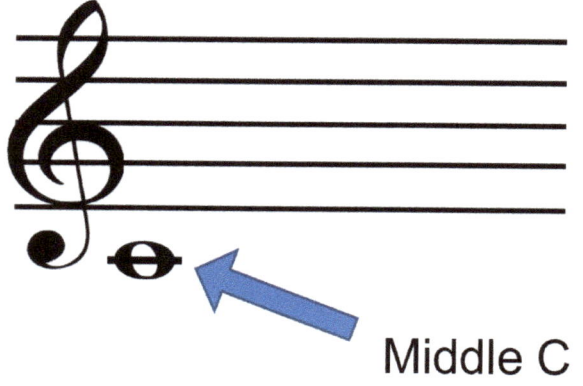

Finger Map

Middle C

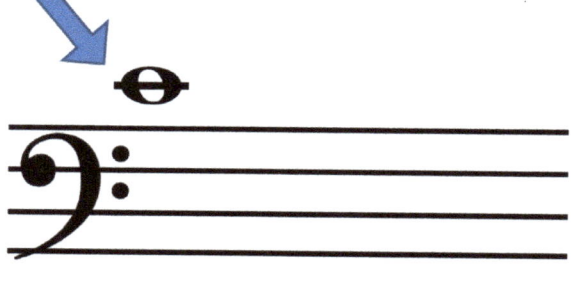

Middle C

Middle C is closer to the bass clef when you are to use your left hand.

Practice!

+ **Clap and count the rhythm of this song**

Middle C Remix

 + **Play this song with a steady beat!**

Treble G

TREBLE G is the first G above middle C.

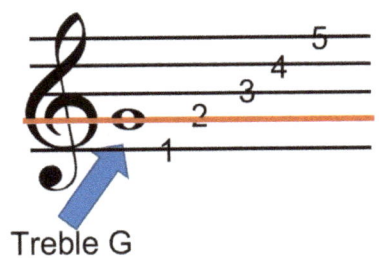

Treble G

Finger Map

Treble G is on the second line on the treble clef.

Practice!

+ **How many middle Cs are in this song?**

+ **Circle all the treble Gs**

Finger Map

Agent of Change

When a note is on the same line or space, it is a repeating note.

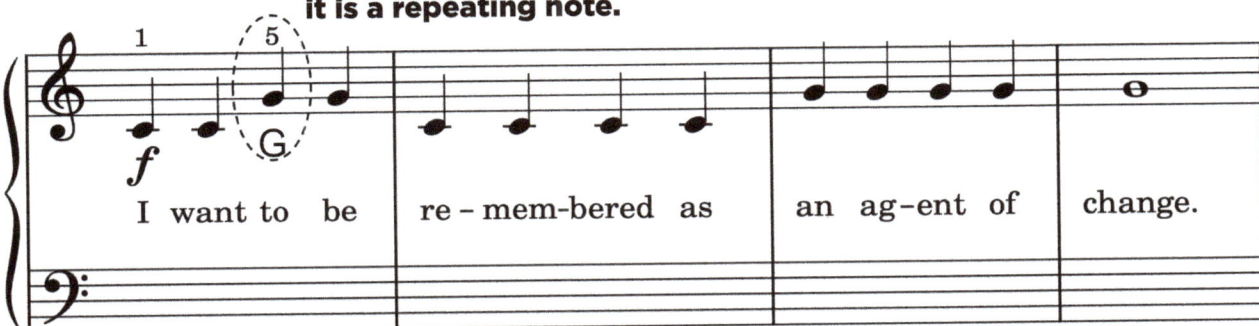

I want to be | re-mem-bered as | an ag-ent of | change.

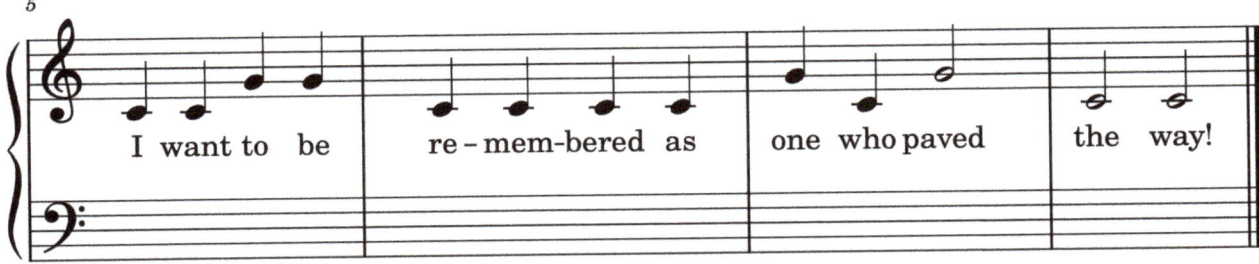

I want to be | re-mem-bered as | one who paved | the way!

Shirley Chisholm

Shirley Chisholm (1924-2005) was born in Brooklyn, New York. She was a politician, educator and author. In 1968, she became the first African American woman in congress. Chisholm was also the first woman and African American to seek nomination for President of The United States. During her seven terms in the U.S. House of Representatives, she was a constant advocate for women and minorities.

Bass F

BASS F is the F below middle C.

 **MEZZO FORTE** (*mf*) means to play moderately loud.

Bass F is on the fourth line on the treble bass.

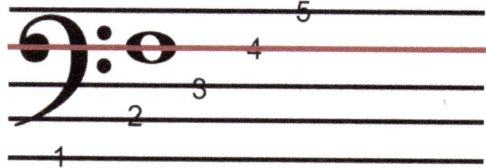

Practice!

+ Circle all the bass Fs
+ Play the song *mf*

Brother and Sister

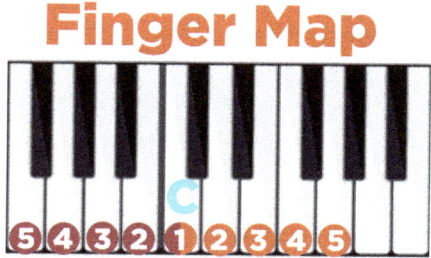

mf

You're my lit tle bro – ther. Some times we do fight.

Play C and G together!

But youre my fav 'rite bro – ther, so we will be al – right!

 When two notes are on top of each other, play them together at the same time.

Practice!

+ **Fill in the missing notes**

Finger Map

Running Out of Time

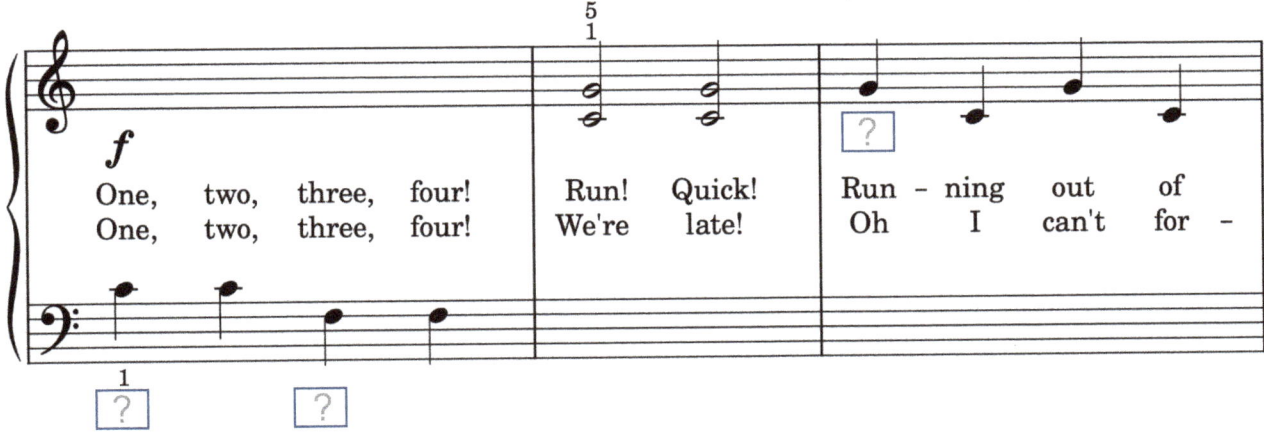

One, two, three, four!
One, two, three, four!

Run! Quick!
We're late!

Run - ning out of
Oh I can't for -

Time!
get!

Lost my socks. My
Grab my bear and

shoes don't fit.
my le gos.

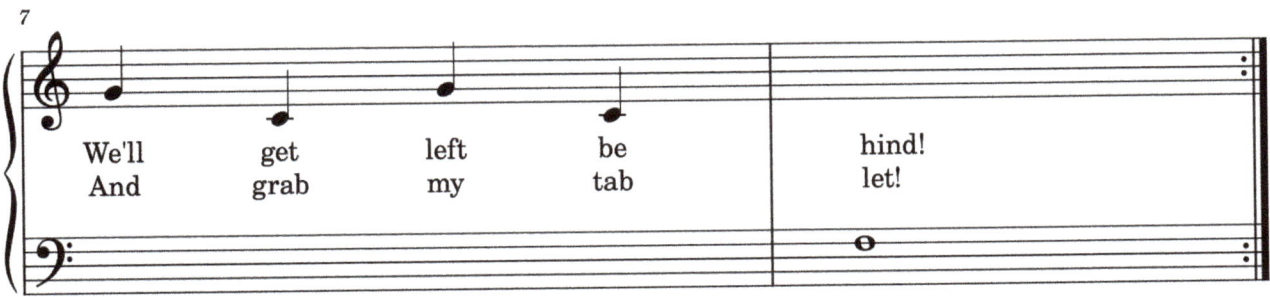

We'll get left be
And grab my tab

hind!
let!

Can you memorize the song?
How quickly can you play the song?

53

Time Signatures

The **TIME SIGNATURE** is written at the beginning of a song. It tells you how many beats are in each measure. It also tells you which notes get one beat.

4
4

The top number tells us how many beats are in a measure. In this example, there are 4 beats.

The bottom number "4" represents quarter notes ♩.
This means quarter notes get one beat.

The time signature is written at the beginning of the staff after the treble or bass clef sign.

Practice!

+ **Trace the time signature**

+ **Fill in the blanks**

4
4

Means _____ beats in a measure

Means _____ get 1 beat
(draw the note)

Review Time!

+ Where is treble G on the music staff?

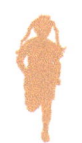

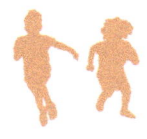

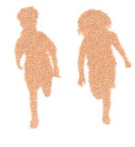

Practice

Don't forget that you only clap once for each note!

+ Practice clapping and counting in $\frac{4}{4}$

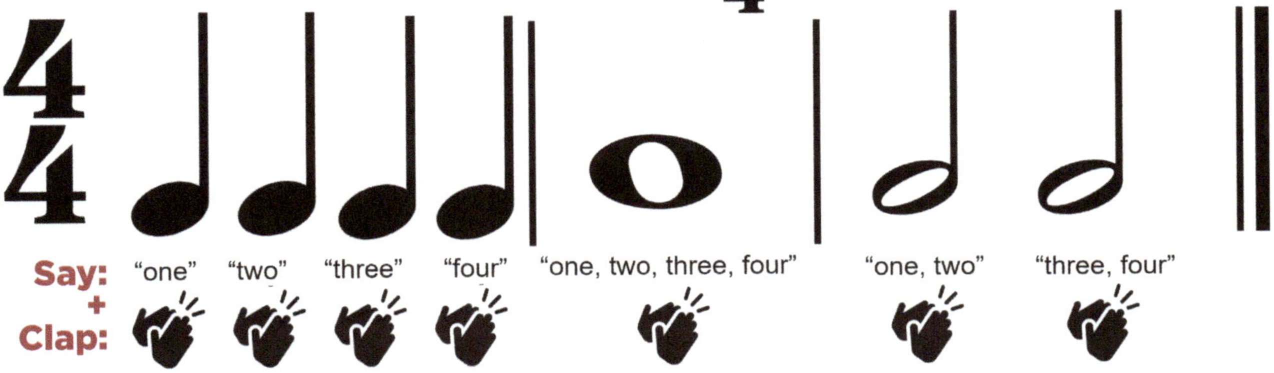
Say:
+
Clap:
"one"
"two"
"three"
"four"
"one, two, three, four"
"one, two"
"three, four"

Notice every measure has four beats!

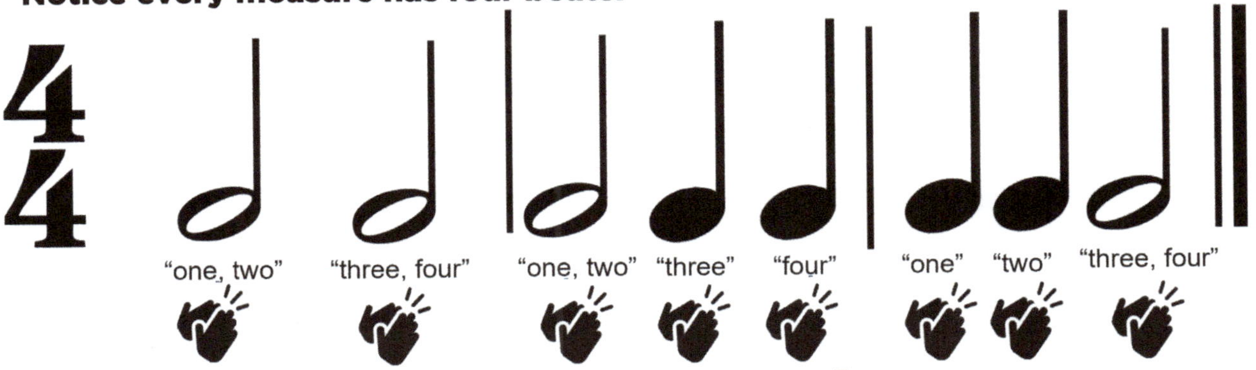
"one, two"
"three, four"
"one, two"
"three"
"four"
"one"
"two"
"three, four"

+ Write out how you would count this rhythm in $\frac{4}{4}$

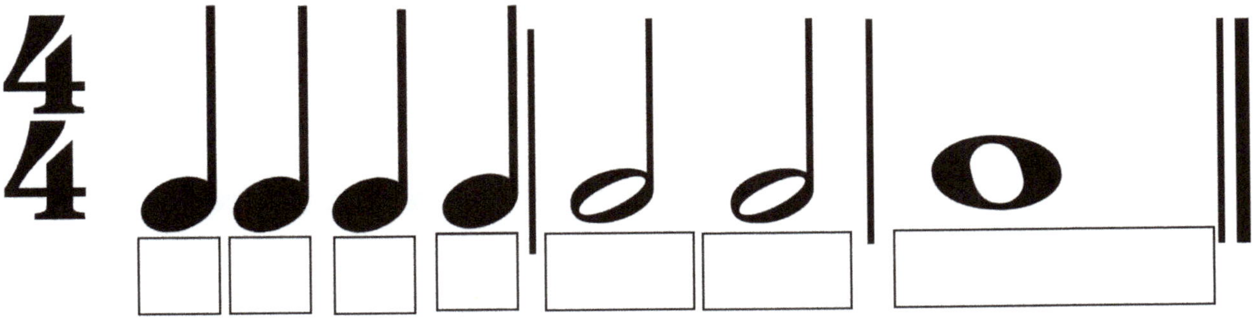

D,E, and F are the 3 notes between C and G. Notice how the letters are in alphabetical order as they go up the treble clef: C,D,E,F, G.

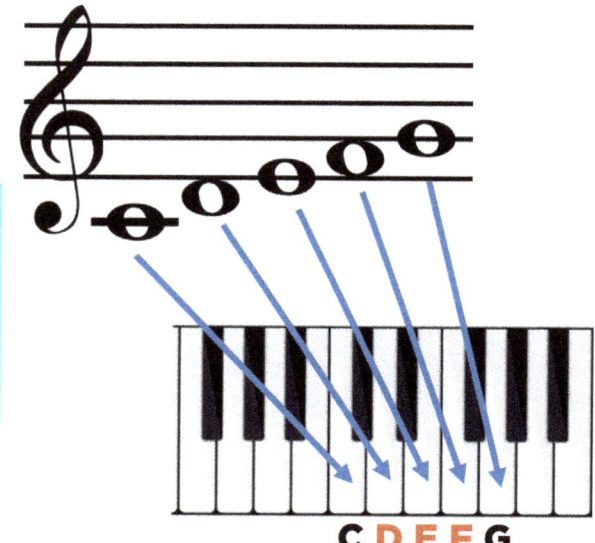

Review Time!

+ **What is a time signature?**

+ **What is the grand staff?**

C D E F G

Practice!

+ **Name the notes**

+ **Count and clap the rhythm in 4/4**

Put it in a Song

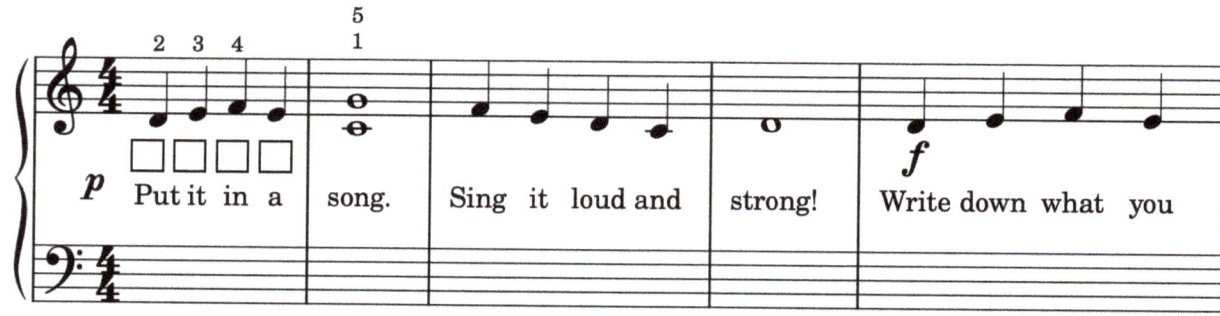

56

In the Spotlight

Nina Simone !

Nina Simone (1933-2003) was born in Tryon, North Carolina. Simone was a performer who sang jazz, blues and folk music in the 1950's and 60's. Because she wrote songs about tragedies in America due to racism, she was known as the voice of the Civil Rights Movement.

Practice!

+ **Name the notes**

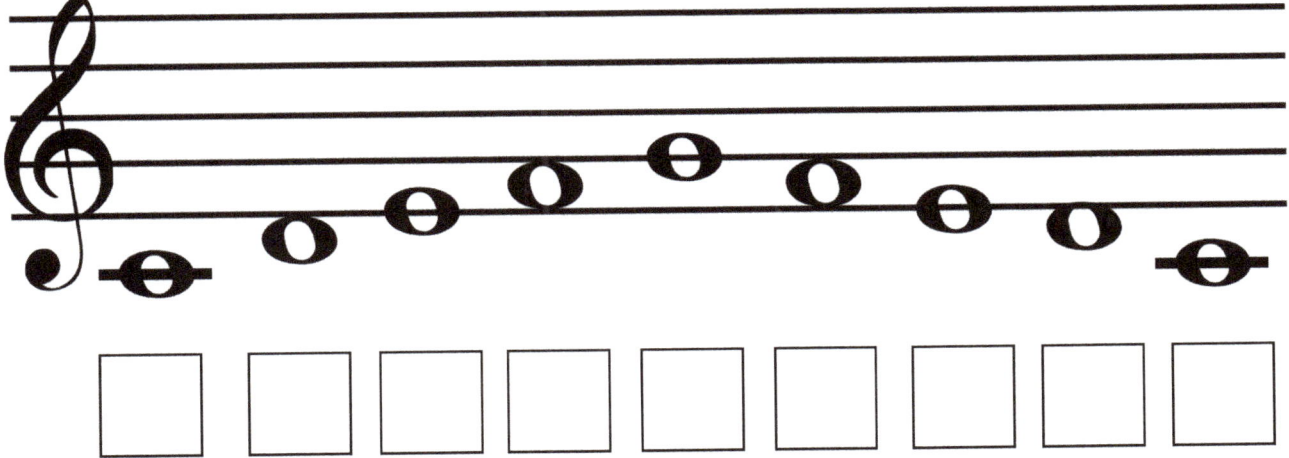

 The notes on the staff go in alphabetical order.

Dotted Half Notes

A **DOTTED HALF NOTE** lasts for 3 beats. That means you will hold down a piano key and count to three.

A dotted half note looks like a half note with a dot to the right of it.

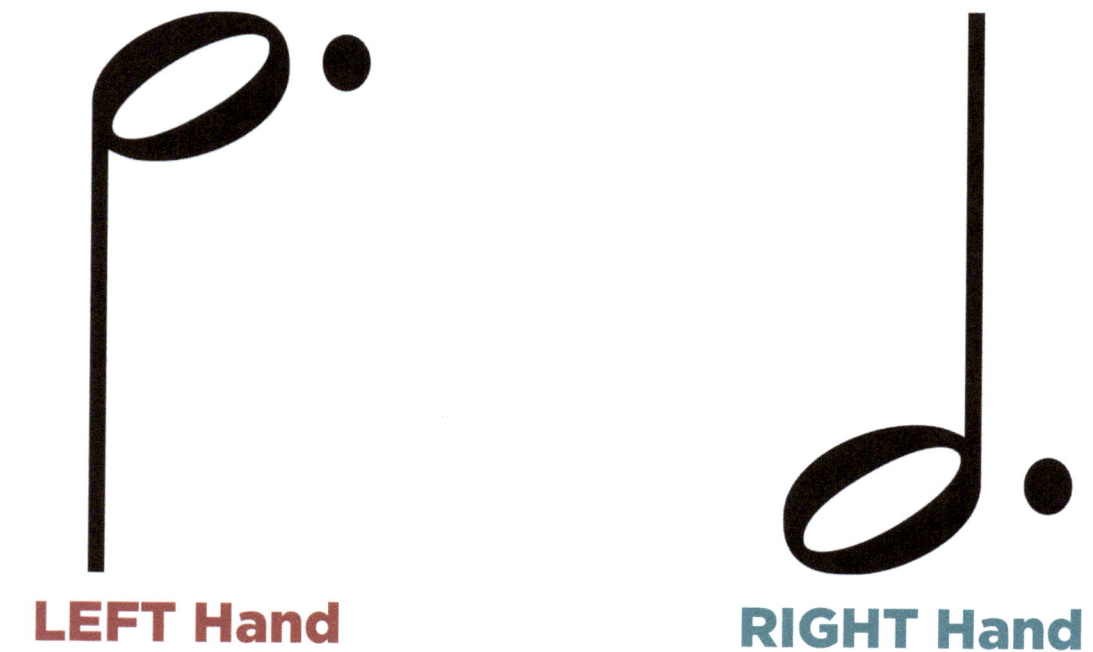

LEFT Hand   **RIGHT Hand**

Practice!

+   **Practice drawing a dotted half note**

Practice!

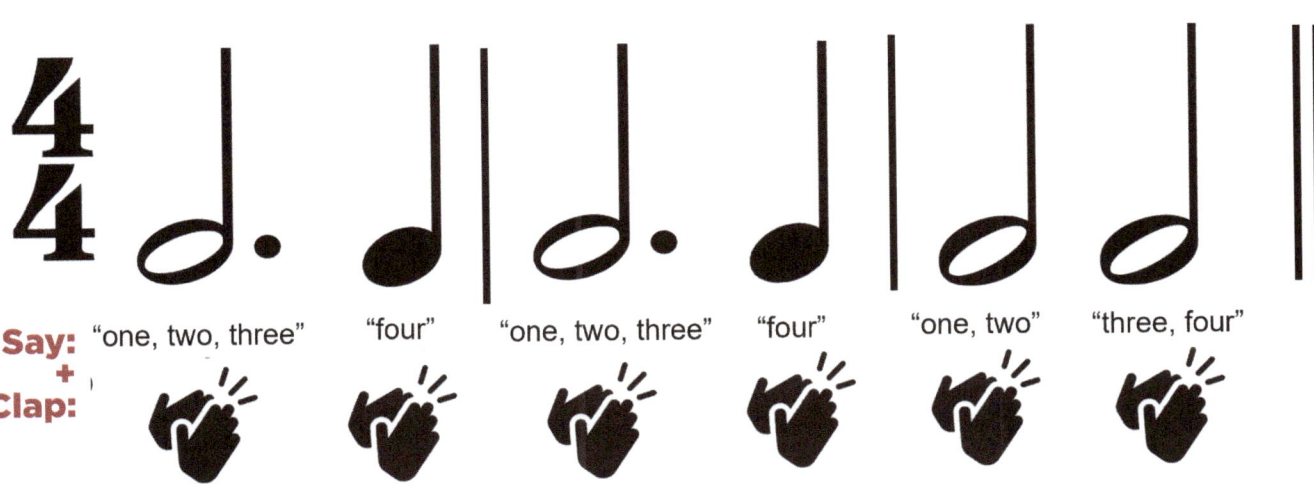

4/4 ♩. ♪ | ♩. ♪ | ♩ ♪ |

Say: "one, two, three" "four" "one, two, three" "four" "one, two" "three, four"
+
Clap:

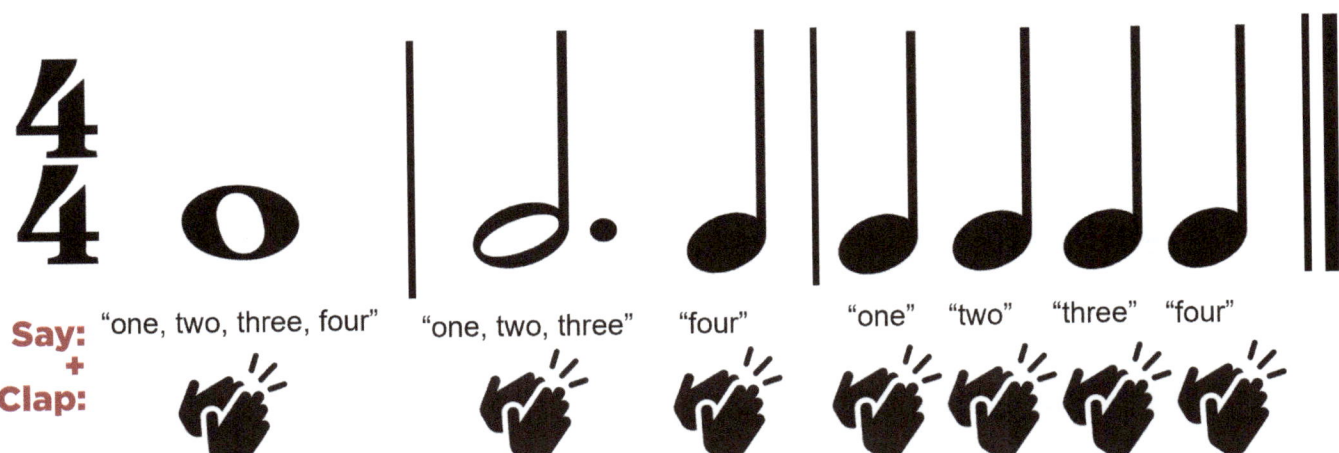

4/4 o | ♩. ♪ | ♪ ♪ ♪ ♪ |

Say: "one, two, three, four" "one, two, three" "four" "one" "two" "three" "four"
+
Clap:

The TIME SIGNATURE is written at the beginning of a song. It tells you how many beats are in each measure.

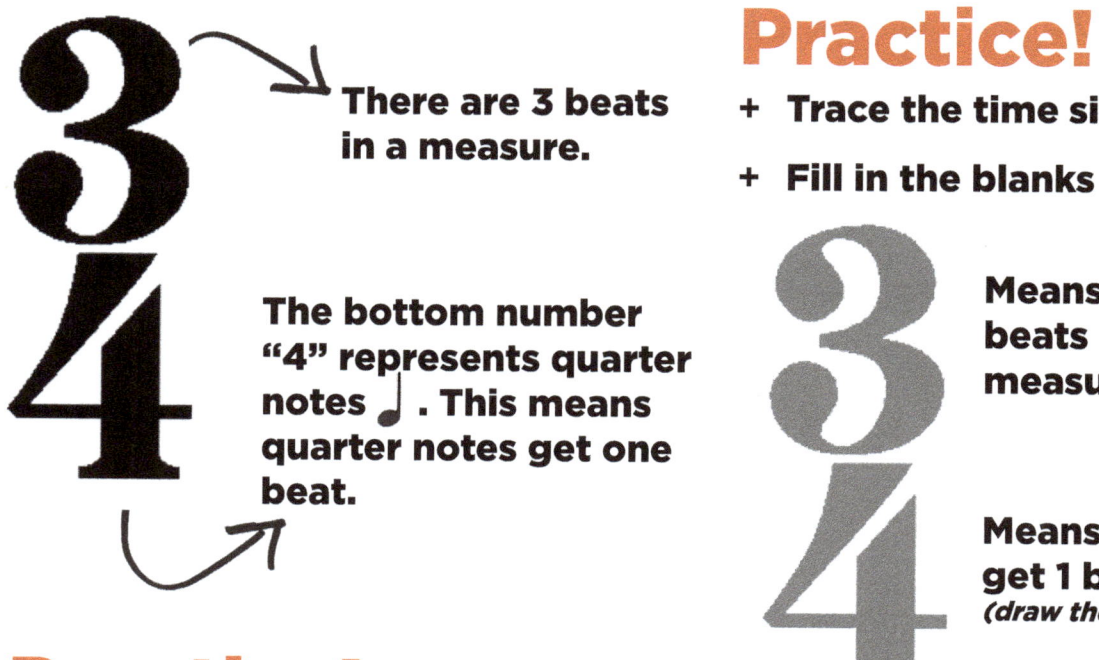

There are 3 beats in a measure.

The bottom number "4" represents quarter notes ♩. This means quarter notes get one beat.

Practice!

+ Trace the time signature
+ Fill in the blanks

Means _____ beats in a measure

Means _____ get 1 beat
(draw the note)

Practice!

+ Practice counting and clapping the rhythm.
+ How many beats are in each measure?

Say: "one, two, three"   "one, two, three"   "one, two"   "three"   "one"   "two"   "three"
+
Clap:

Don't forget to repeat!

60

Review Time!

+ How many beats are in a measure when playing in $\frac{3}{4}$?
+ What is *mf*?

Practice!

+ **Circle the time signature**
+ **Clap and count the rhythm in $\frac{3}{4}$**
+ **How many beats are in each measure?**

Finger Map

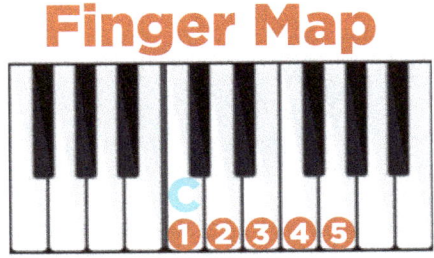

Watch Out for the Dot!

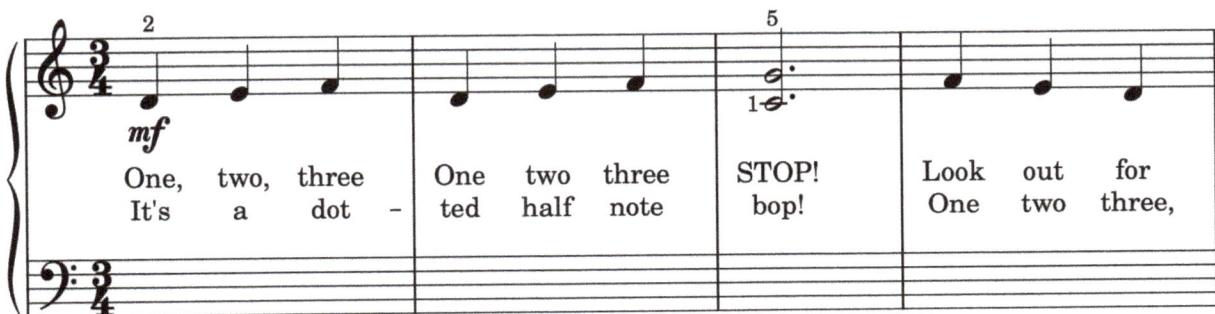

One, two, three   One two three   STOP!   Look out for
It's a dot -   ted half note   bop!   One two three,

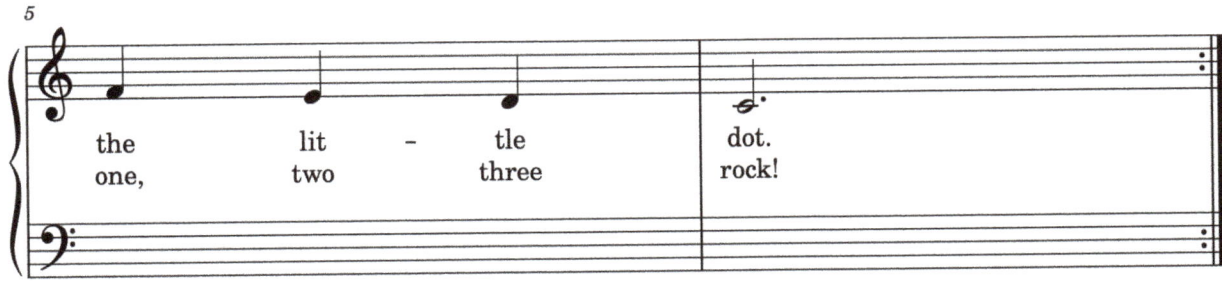

the lit - tle   dot.
one, two three   rock!

Randy J. Gibson

Professor Randy J. Gibson was born in Atlanta, Georgia. He is a prolific concert pianist, composer and recording artist, who has performed throughout the world. Along with his wife, Wilhemina Gibson, they founded the Gibson School of Music & Arts in 1995, where they have nurtured several generations of talented musicians including the author of this book! Many of his students have experienced much success receiving Grammys, Emmys, Tony's and more!

Finger Map

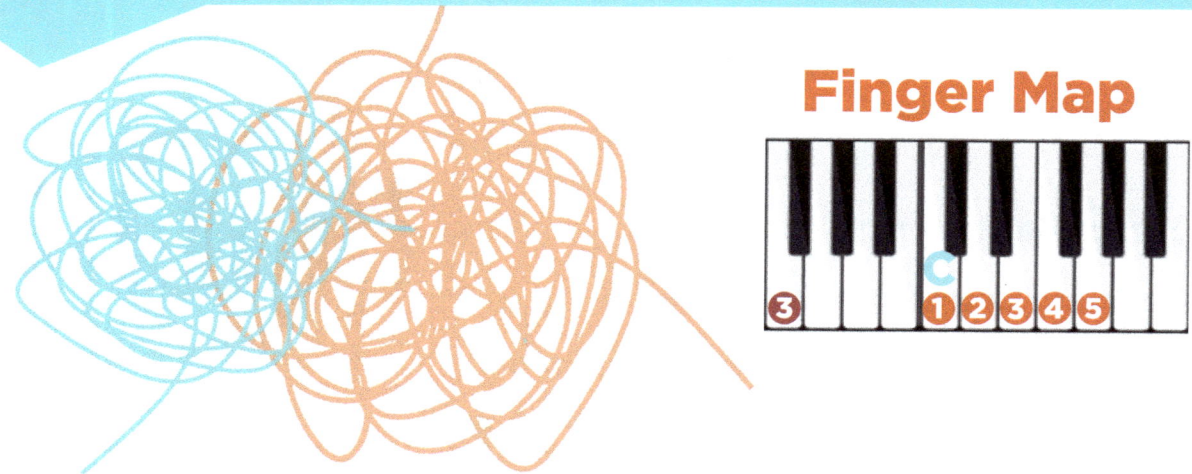

Come and Take a Ride

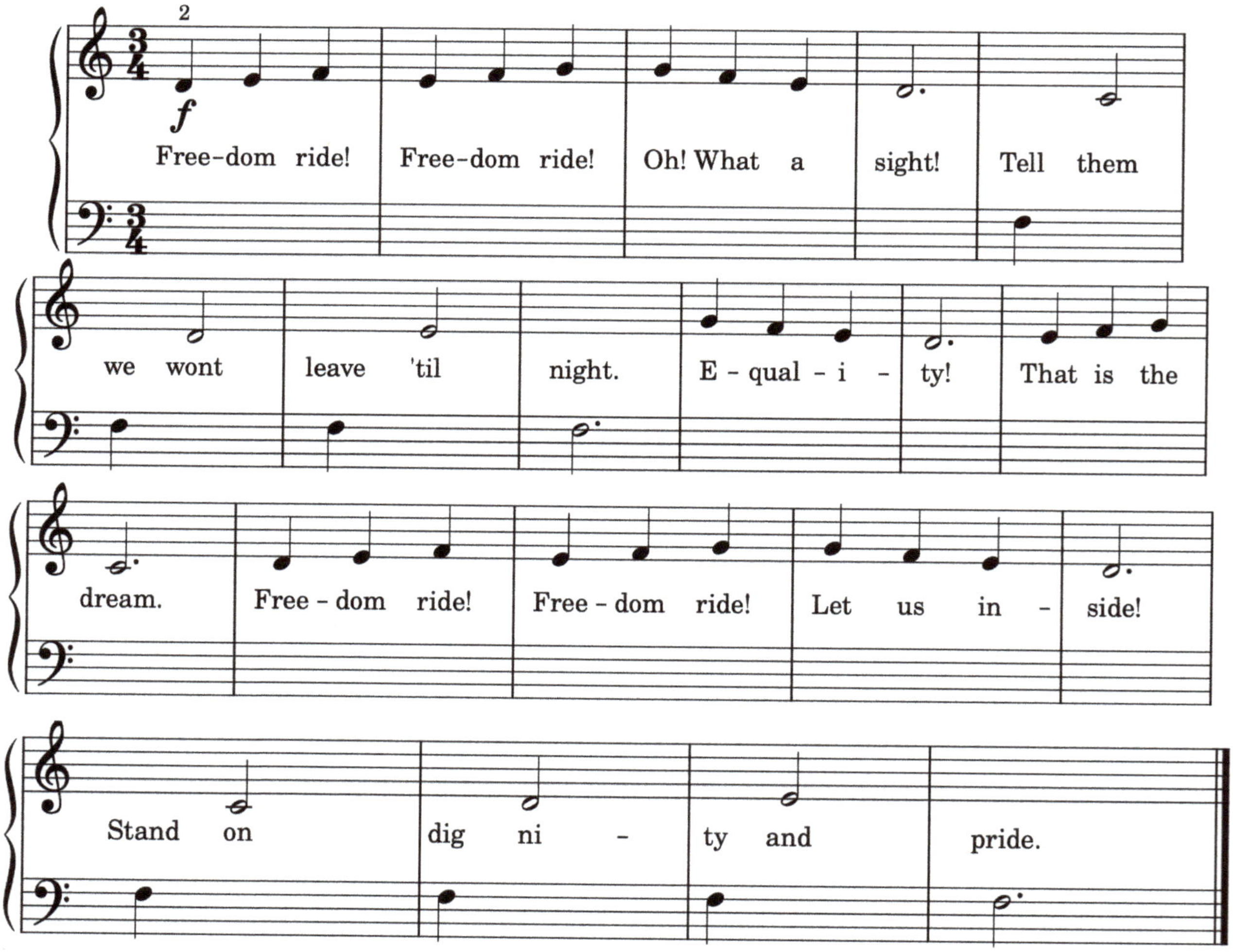

Free-dom ride! Free-dom ride! Oh! What a sight! Tell them

we wont leave 'til night. E - qual - i - ty! That is the

dream. Free - dom ride! Free - dom ride! Let us in - side!

Stand on dig ni - ty and pride.

James Farmer

James Farmer (1920-1999) was born in Marshall, Texas. Farmer was one of the "Big Four." The Big Four was a term the press used to describe Farmer, Dr. Martin Luther King, Jr., and Whitney Young, during the Civil Rights Movement. As a civil rights activist he used non-violent techniques such as sit-ins and peaceful demonstrations. In 1961, he organized the Freedom Rides throughout The South to desegregate bus travel.

Practice!

+ **Name the notes**

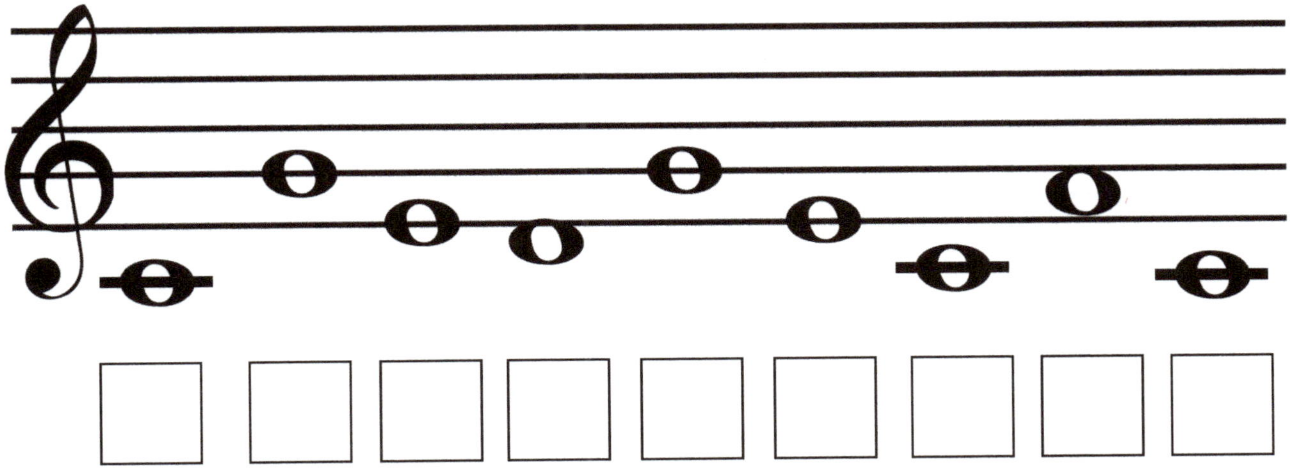

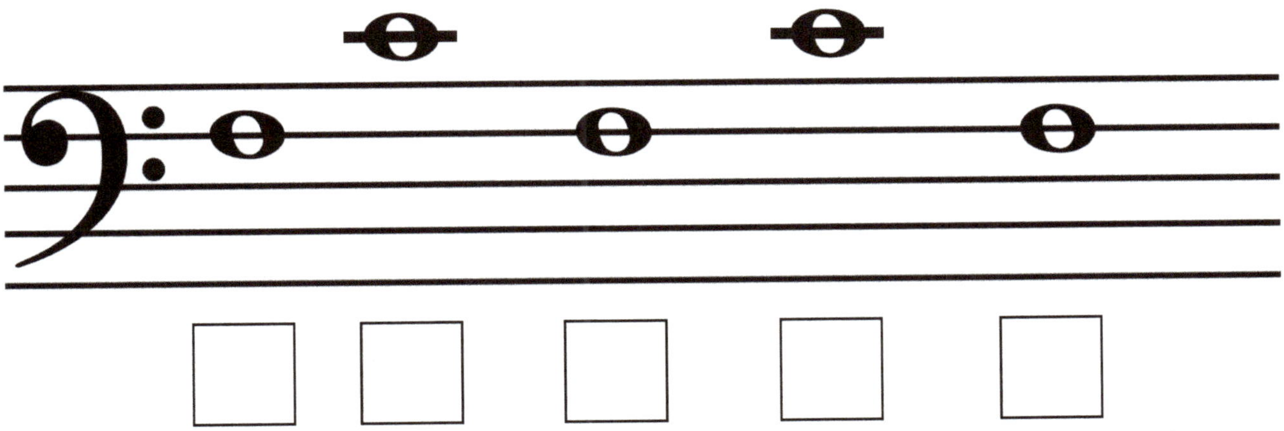

Legato

LEGATO means to play in a **SMOOTH** and **CONNECTED** way. When you play legato, you won't hear any breaks in the sound.

To do this, one finger goes down just as the other finger comes up. Think of the smooth motion of a rocking chair.

A **SLUR** is a curved line over or under a group of notes. When you see this symbol, you are to play legato.

Practice!

+ Trace all the slurs in this song

+ How many slurs are there?

+ Play the song slowly and listen for a smooth and connected sound

Simply Smooth

On the bass clef, the notes between bass F and middle C are G, A, and B.

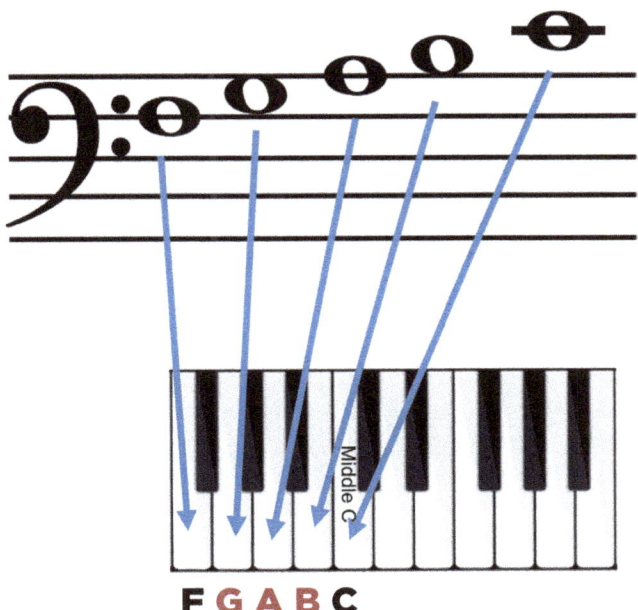

F G A B C

B

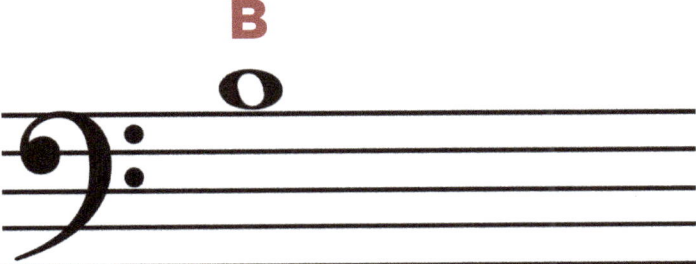

B is the note below middle C on the keyboard.

B is a space note and sits on top of the bass clef.

B

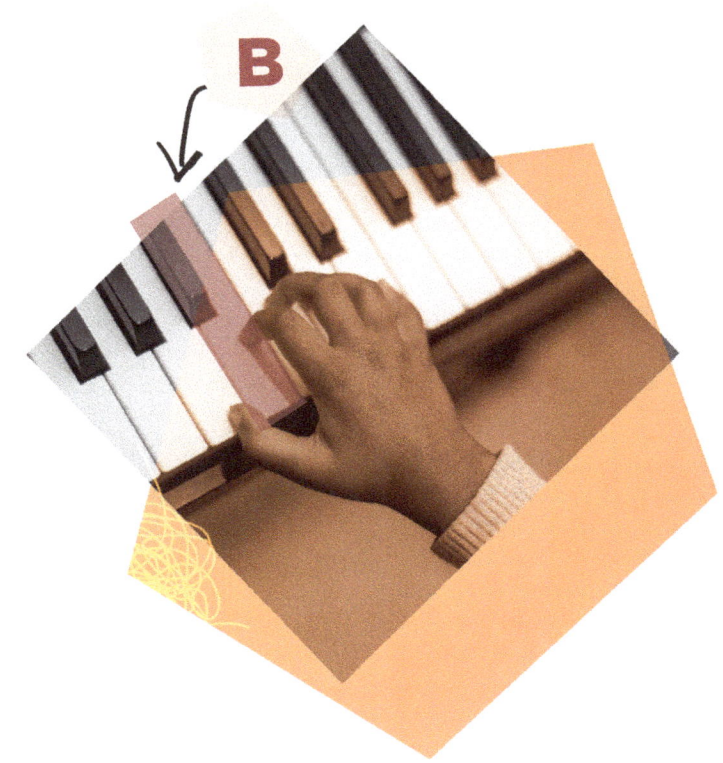

Practice!

+ **Circle all the Bs in the song**
+ **Trace all slurs**
+ **Fill in the missing notes**

Finger Map

The Queen Bey

Happily

Ev - 'ry bo - dy / please make way! / Make way for the / Queen!.
When I grow up / I can be / an y thing I / dream!

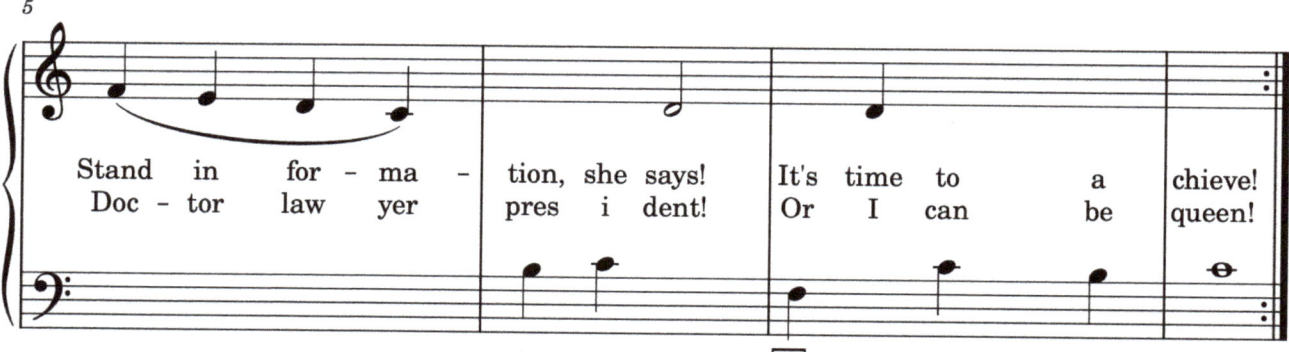

Stand in for - ma - / tion, she says! / It's time to a / chieve!
Doc - tor law yer / pres i dent! / Or I can be / queen!

Beyonce Knowles

Beyonce Giselle Knowles (1981) was born in Houston, Texas. She is a singer, songwriter, record producer, actress and philanthropist. Known lovingly by her fans as "Queen Bey," she is one of the most influential and successful musicians today. Songs such as "Formation" and "Who Run the World?" and her album "Black is King" address women empowerment, activism in the Black community and celebration of Black life. Beyonce has used her success to create initiatives all across the world to help underserved populations.

66

A is the top line note on the bass clef. It is on line 5.

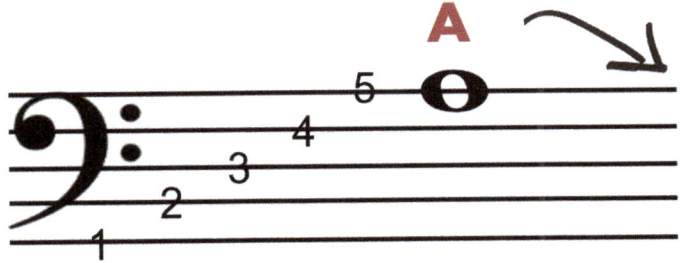
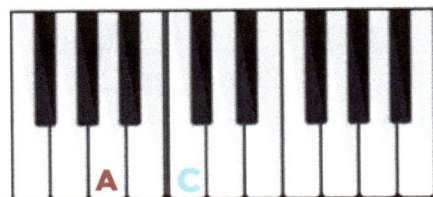

Practice!

+ **Circle all the As**

+ **Trace the slur**

Finger Map

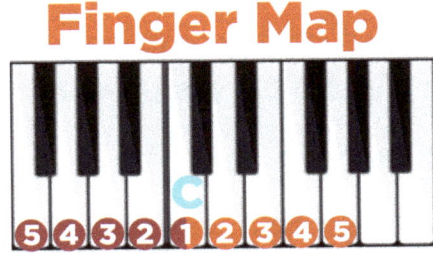

Rainy Day

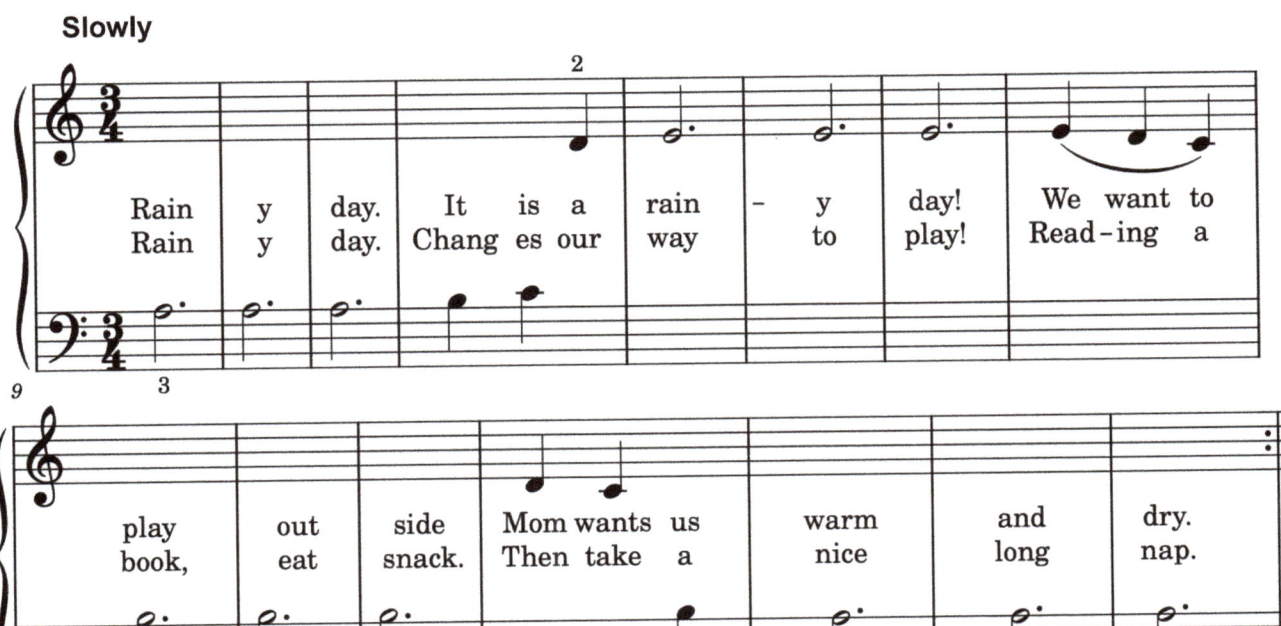

Slowly

Rain y day. It is a rain - y day! We want to
Rain y day. Chang es our way to play! Read-ing a

play out side Mom wants us warm and dry.
book, eat snack. Then take a nice long nap.

Review Time!

+ **Where is A on the bass clef? B?**

G is space 4 on the bass clef.

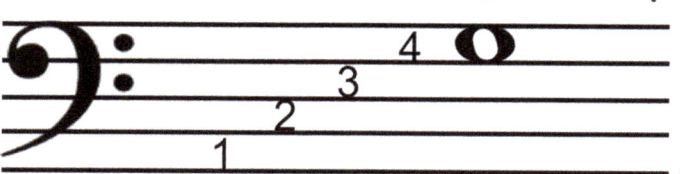

Practice!

+ **Circle all the Gs on the bass clef**

+ **Trace the slur**

After Church

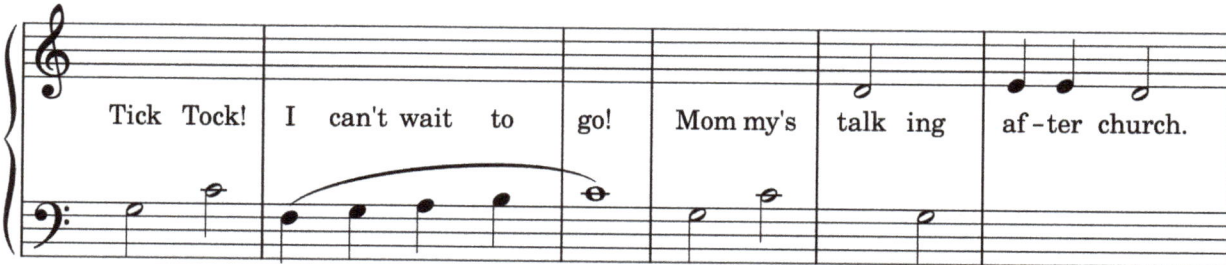

Unit 5

Intervals

Seconds

An **INTERVAL** is the distance between 2 notes.

The intervals you will learn are called **SECONDS**, **THIRDS**, **FOURTHS**, **FIFTHS**, and **OCTAVES**.

Playing a second (also known as a step) is going from one note to the next one above or below it.

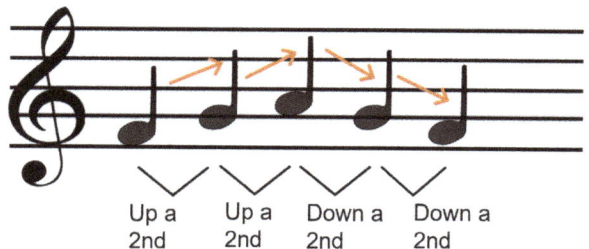

Going from C to D is up →a second. Playing a G and then an F is going down ← a second.

On a music staff a second is written as a space note going to a **LINE NOTE** OR a line note going to a **SPACE NOTE**.

Practice!

+ Write up (U) or down (D) for each group of seconds

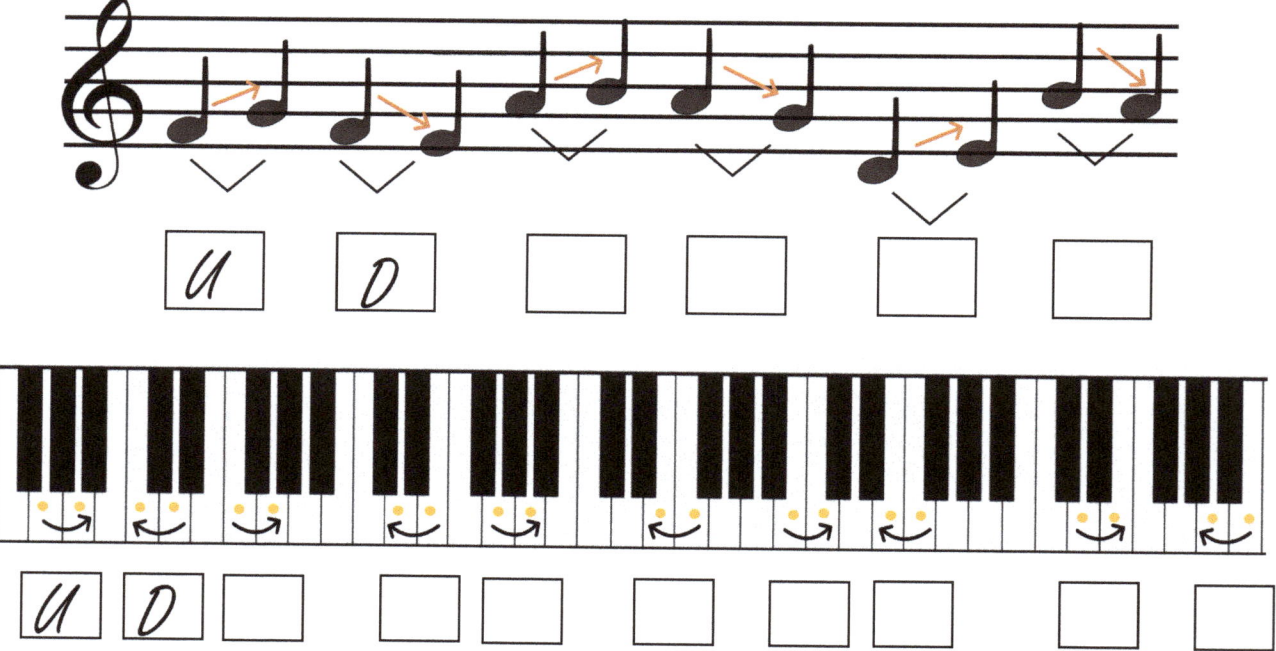

70

+ **What is a second?**

+ **What is legato?**

Practice!

+ **Draw arrows to show if a note is going up a second or down a second.**

Finger Map

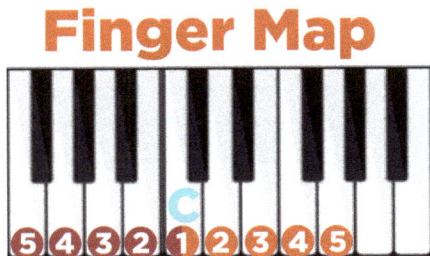

Give it a Second Try

Slowly

2   *Down a second*

I   may   not   have   it   on   the   first   try   but   I   will
There is   a   sec - ret my dad dy   tells me when I

f

3   *Up a second*

4

try   a   gain.   Do not count me   out of the game be cause I   am
am with him.   It's not how man   y times you fall but how man y

8

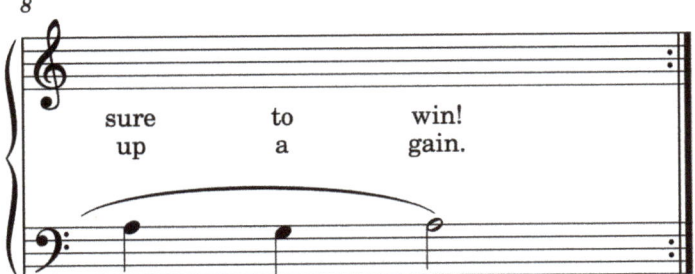

sure   to   win!
up   a   gain.

Bass C

BASS C is a space note. It is space 2 on the bass clef. It is the C below middle C on your piano or keyboard.

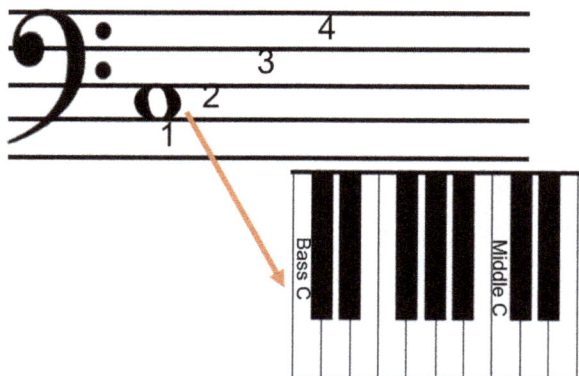

Practice!

+ **Circle all the bass C's**

+ **Trace all the slurs**

Finger Map

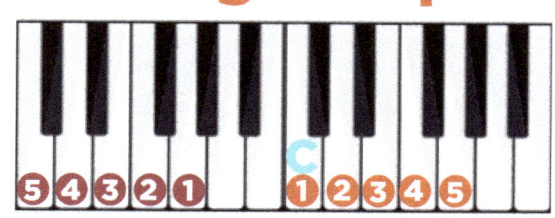

Malcolm's Tale

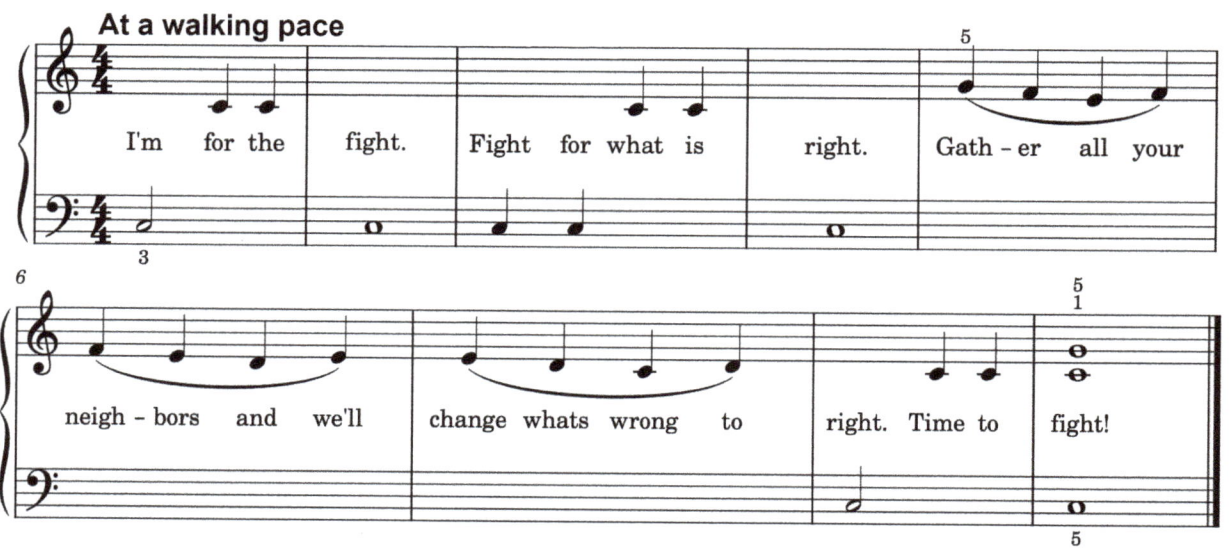

At a walking pace

I'm   for the | fight. | Fight for what is | right. | Gath – er   all your

neigh – bors   and   we'll | change whats wrong   to | right. Time to | fight!

Play left and right hand together

Malcolm X

Malcolm X (1925-1965) originally named Malcolm Little, was born in Omaha, Nebraska. He was a civil rights activist. He believed that African Americans should fight for their rights by "any means necessary." Malcolm X was known for his association with the Nation of Islam. He was admired for his endless striving to build black pride and racial unity across the world. He was assassinated on February 21, 1965.

Thirds

THIRDS are another type of interval. To play a third, also known as a skip, you must skip one key.

On the music staff, a third is written as a space note going to the next space OR a line note going to the next line.

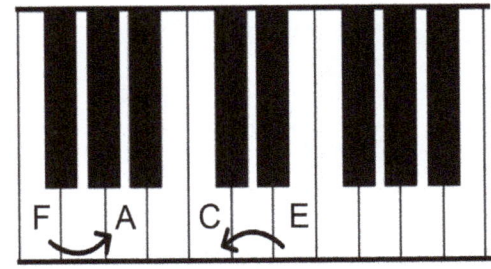

Going from F to A is up → a third. Playing a C and then an E is going down ← a third.

Space to Space

Up a 3rd   Up a 3rd

Line to Line

Down a 3rd   Down a 3rd

Practice!

+ **Draw a circle on the key that is a third above**

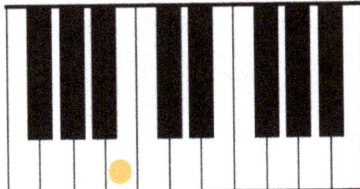

+ **Name the intervals**

 Thirds are from line to line OR space to space

2nd

+ What is a second?
+ What is a third?

Practice!

+ Circle the time signature
+ Trace the arrows
+ Circle the groups of thirds

Finger Map

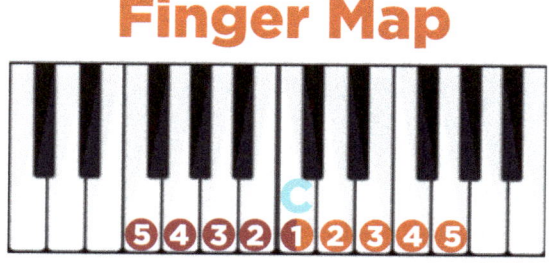

The Skip Anthem

Lively and Fast

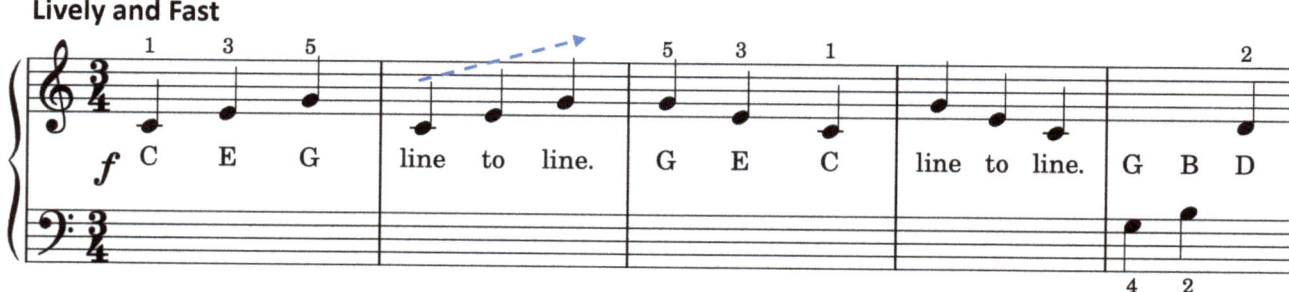

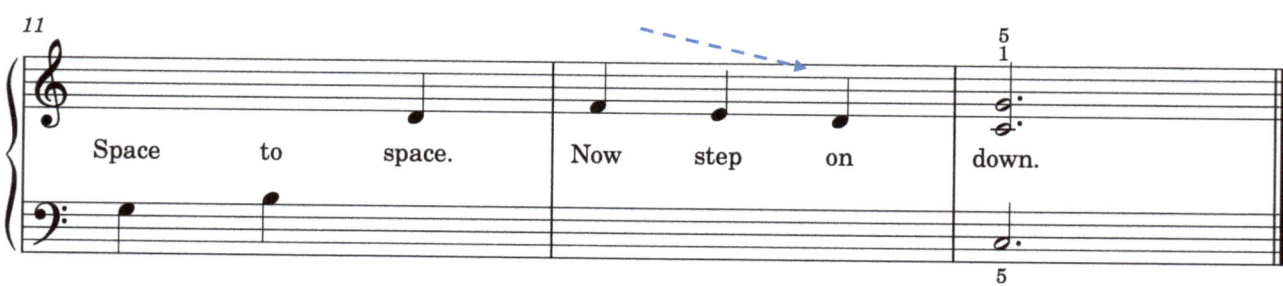

?

+ **Which interval goes from line to space on the staff?**

+ **Where is bass C on the bass clef?**

+ **How many beats does a half note get?**

D is line 3 on the bass clef. It is the white key after bass C

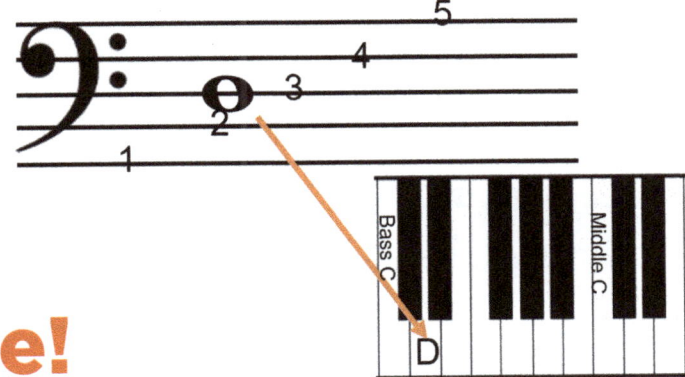

Practice!

+ **Circle all the D's on the bass clef**

+ **Fill in the missing note names**

Watch out for dynamics! (*f*, *p*)

Finger Map

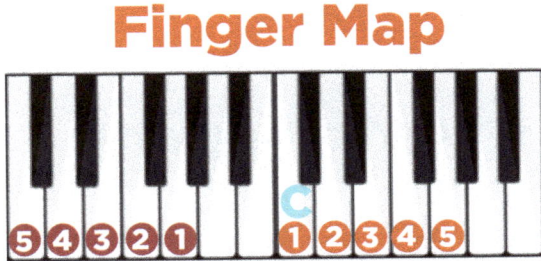

Echo Forest

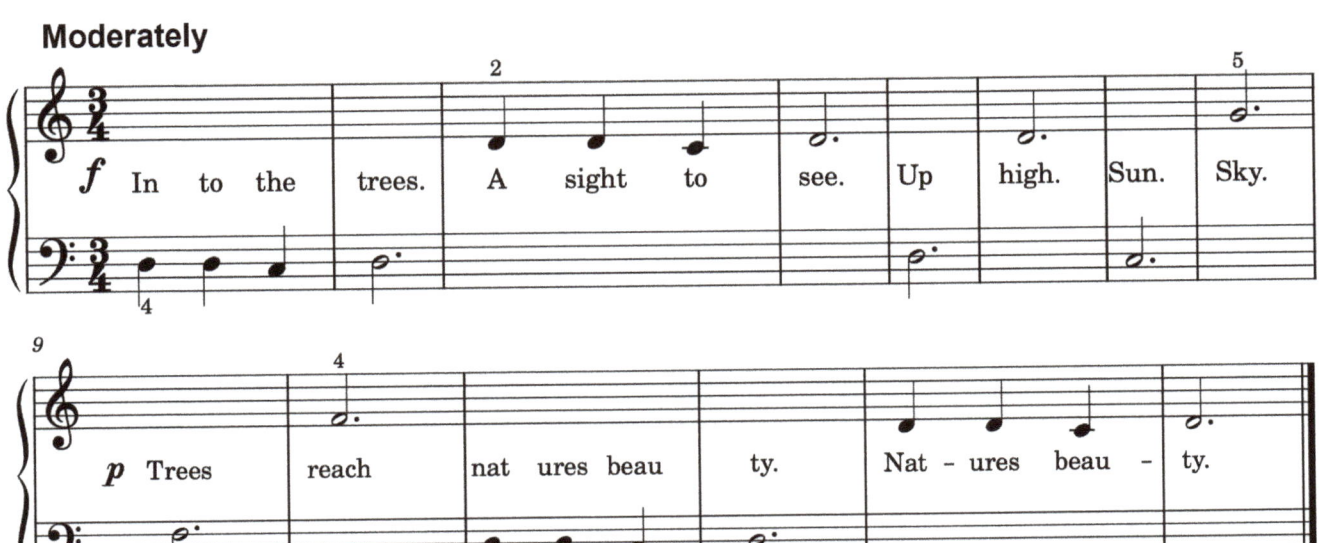

Moderately

f In to the trees. A sight to see. Up high. Sun. Sky.

p Trees reach nat ures beau ty. Nat - ures beau - ty.

?

+ **Which interval goes from line to space on the staff?**

+ **Where is bass C on the bass clef?**

+ **How many beats does a half note get?**

E is on space 3 of the bass clef. It is a third (skip) above bass C.

A **PENTASCALE** is a series of 5 notes in alphabetical order. The **C MAJOR PENTASCALE** is C,D,E,F, and G.

Finger Map

Practice!

+ **Circle all the E's on the bass clef**

+ **How many thirds are there?**

+ **Fill in the note names**

+ **Play this song as a warmup daily**

C Major Pentascale Warm Up

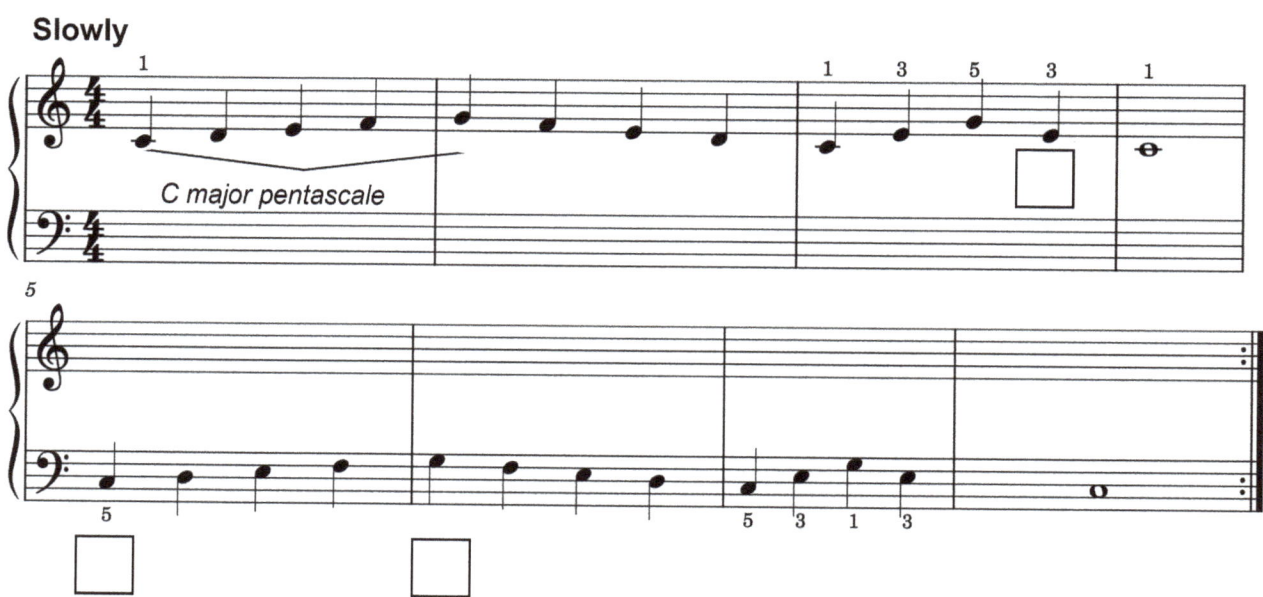

Slowly

C major pentascale

76

Review Time!

+ **What notes are in the C major pentascale?**
+ **Where is E on the bass clef?**

Practice!

+ **Circle the C major pentascales**
+ **Fill in note names**

Ode to Joy

Finger Map

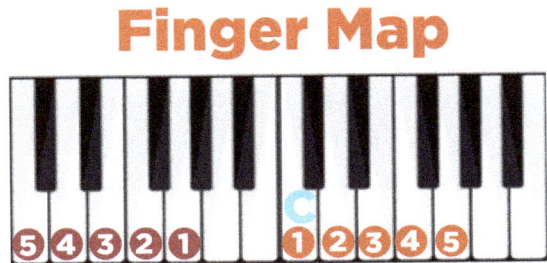

Ludwig van Beethoven
Adapted

Moderately

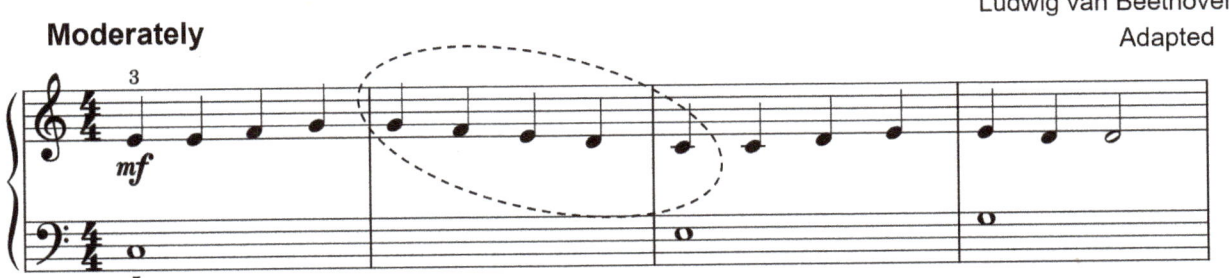

Practice!

+ **Circle the C major pentascales.**

Finger Map

Make a Difference

Lively

$\boldsymbol{f}$ Mak – ing sure that | it's fair. | Show – ing the world | you care!

Take your pass – ion | use it | for the | good. | $\boldsymbol{p}$ Find ing worth in | ev 'ry one!

Take a look at | what you've done. | $\boldsymbol{f}$ Make a diff' ence | even if it is

one small | thing.

LeBron James

LeBron James (1984) was born in Akron, Ohio. He is regarded as one of the greatest basketball players of all time. He is also a social activist and philanthropist who uses his platform and many resources to speak against racial injustice and support underprivileged families and at-risk youth.

When two notes are played separately,
it is called a **MELODIC INTERVAL**.

When two notes are played together,
it is called a **HARMONIC INTERVAL**.

When notes are placed on top of each other
they are harmonic intervals and to be played together.

Melodic Intervals

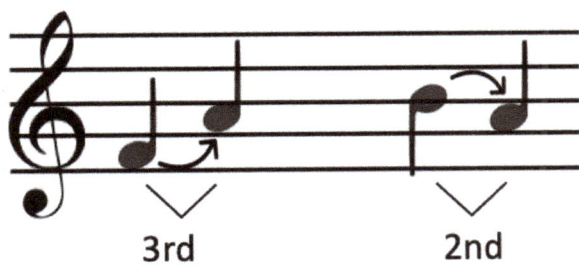

3rd   2nd

Harmonic Intervals

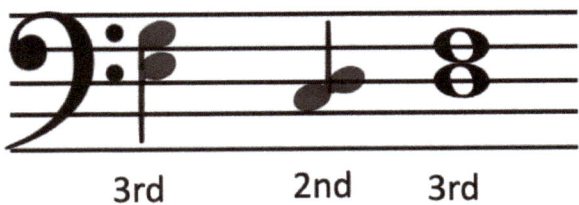

3rd   2nd   3rd

Practice!

+ **Fill in note names**

+ **Play harmonic intervals firmly and slowly**

Finger Map

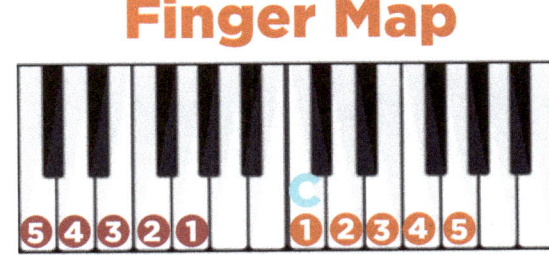

Harmonic Intervals

Slow and steady

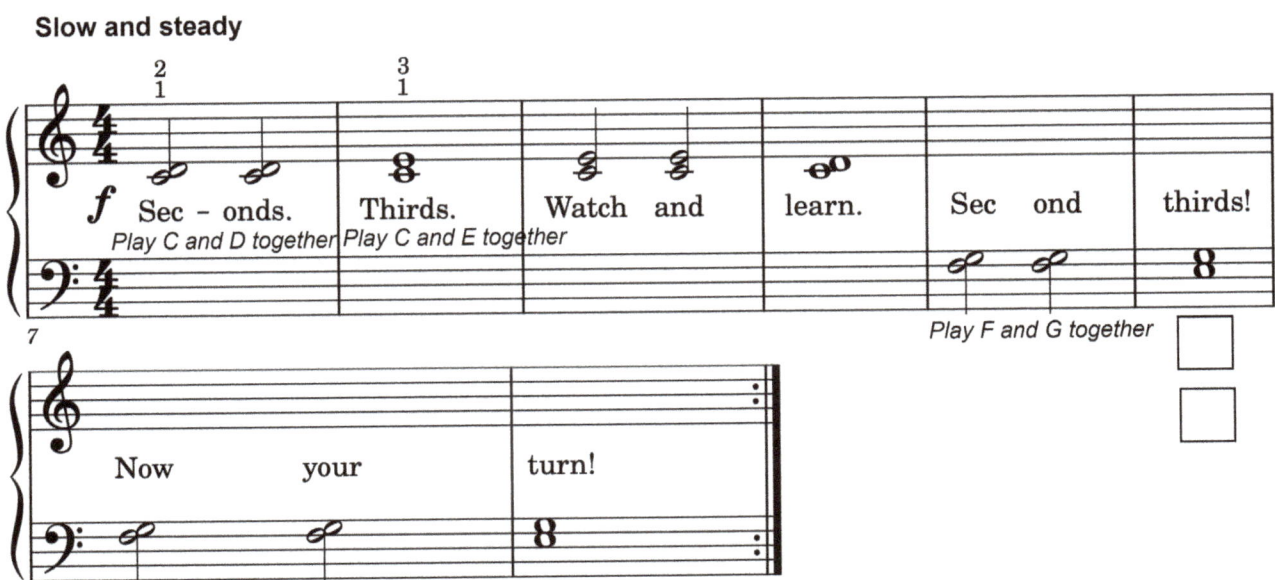

+ **What is a harmonic interval?**
+ **What is a melodic interval?**

A **TRIAD** has 3 notes and is made of thirds.

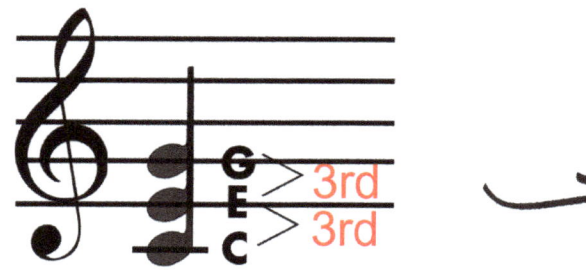

When notes C, E, and G are played together, it is called a **C MAJOR TRIAD**.

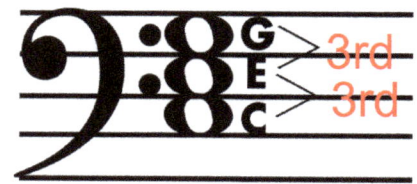

Practice!

+ **Circle the C major triads**
+ **Practice playing a C major triad with your right hand, then left hand**
+ **Fill in the note names**

Finger Map

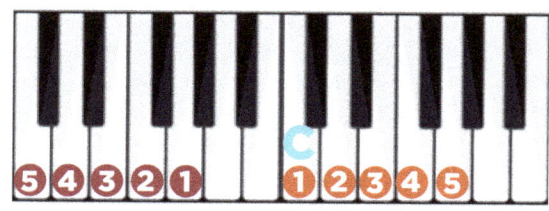

Harmony

Fourths

A **FOURTH** is played when you skip 2 white keys. It can be played as a melodic interval or a harmonic interval.

On a music staff a fourth is written as a space note going to a line note OR a line note going to a space note.

Going from C to F is up → a fourth. Playing a G and then a D is going down ← a fourth.

Line to Space

Up a 4th

Space to Line

Down a 4th

Practice!

+ Draw a circle on the key that is a fourth below

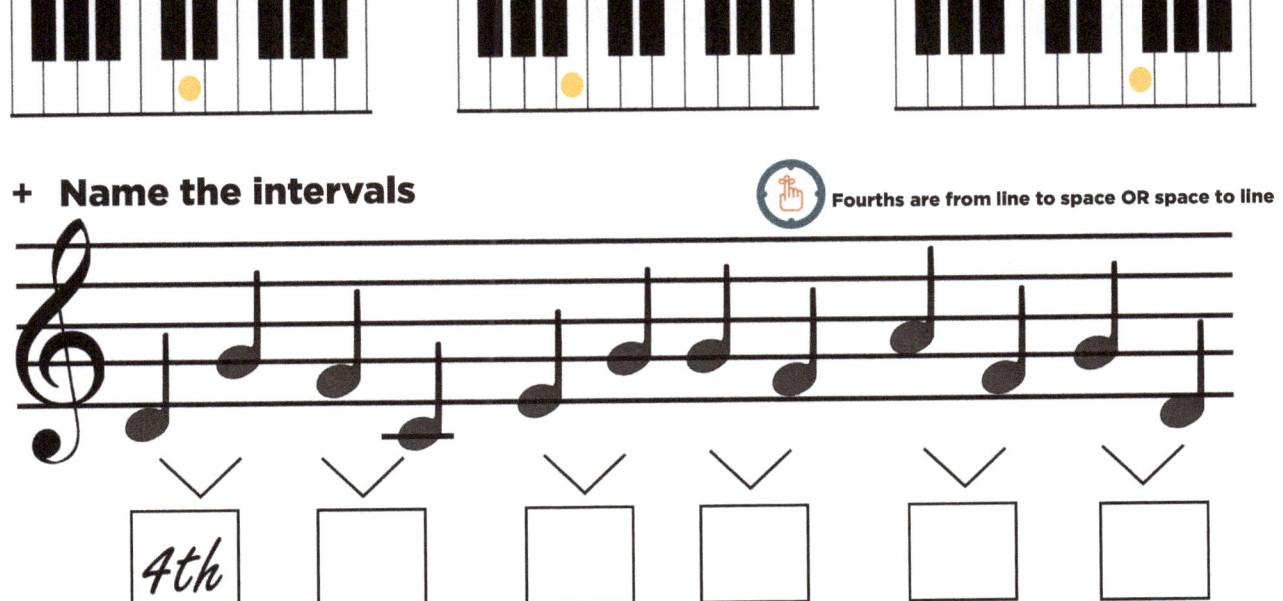

+ Name the intervals

Fourths are from line to space OR space to line

| 4th | | | | | |

81

Practice!

+ Circle the melodic fourths

 Practice song slowly and gradually increase speed

Back and Fourth

Lively

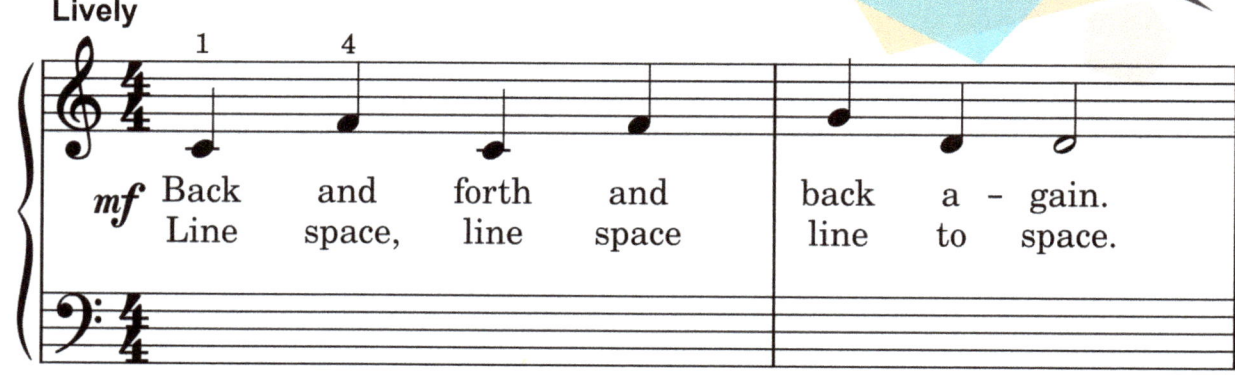

Back and forth and back a - gain.
Line and space, line and space line to space.

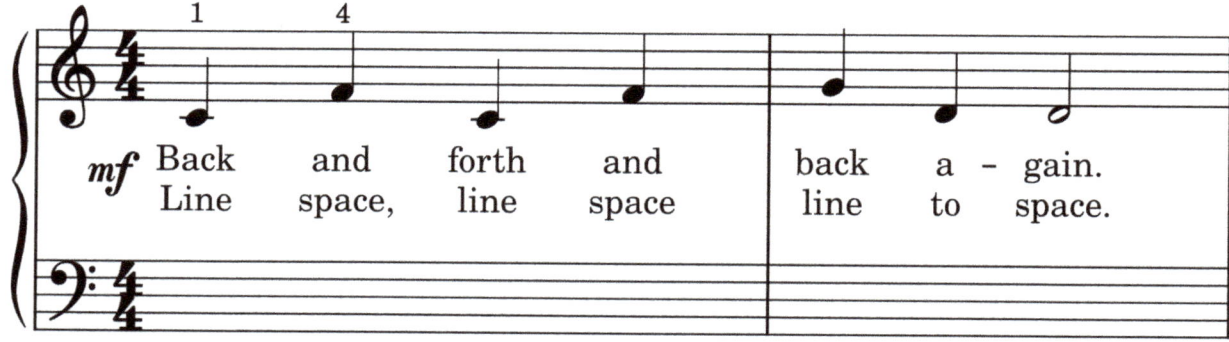

Back and forth and back a - gain.
Line and space, line and space line to space.

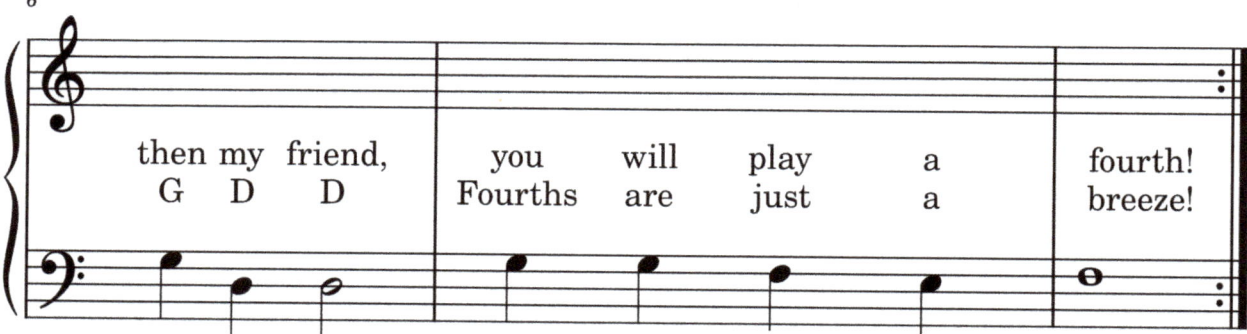

then my friend, you will play a fourth!
G D D Fourths are just a breeze!

Finger Map

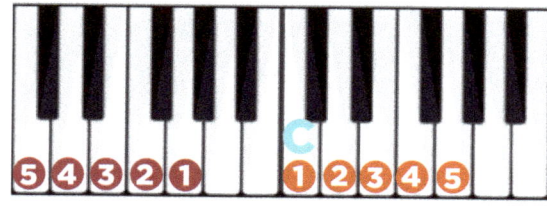

Harmonic Fourths

Practice!

+ **Name the harmonic intervals in the bass clef**

+ **Circle the C major triad**

+ **Play LH alone, then RH alone**

+ **Play both hands together**

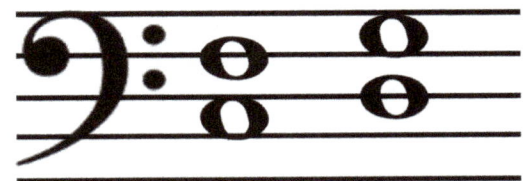

Practice song slowly and gradually increase speed

Finger Map

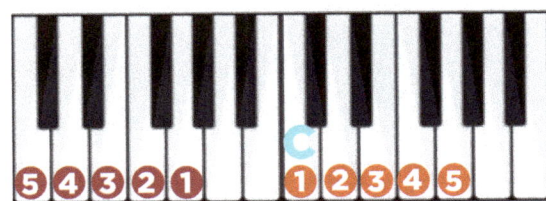

Cleaning My Room

Moderately

1

mf When my | room is | too mess-y to | find | my own

6

1
3

1
2

3rd

1
4

floor then | I know that it's | time! | Toys, | sheets,

11

clothes, | cleats! | Toss it in the | clos-et then I'm | done!

1
3
5

83

Fifths

A **FIFTH** is played when you skip 3 white keys. It can be played as a melodic interval or a harmonic interval.

On a music staff a fifth is written as a space note going to a space note OR a line note going to a line note.

Playing an A and then a D is going down ← a fifth. Going from C to G is up → a fifth.

Line to Line

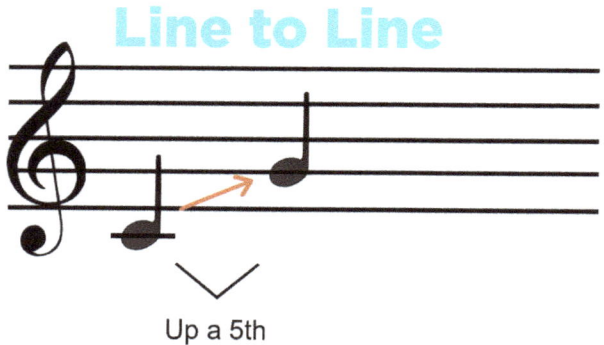

Up a 5th

Space to Space

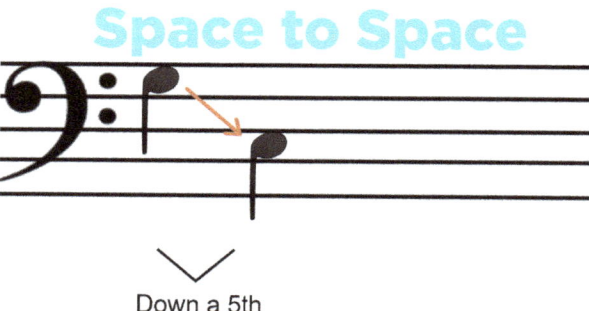

Down a 5th

Practice!

+ **Draw a circle on the key that is a fifth above**

Skip three white keys

+ **Name the intervals**

Fifths are from line to line OR space to space

| 5th | | | | | |

Review Time!

+ **What note is a 5th above C?**
+ **What note is a 5th below A?**

Practice!

+ **Circle the melodic fifths**
+ **Fill in note names**

Finger Map

Sweet Dreams

Slowly

Shift LH hand up   *Shift LH back down*

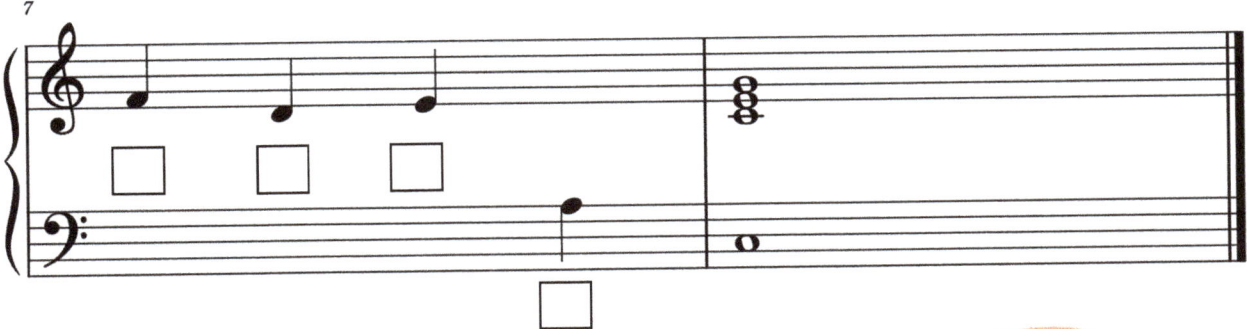

Get Creative!
+ **Make your own song with fifths!**

Harmonic Fifths

Practice!

+ **Trace the slurs**
+ **Circle the harmonic 5ths**
+ **Name the harmonic intervals**

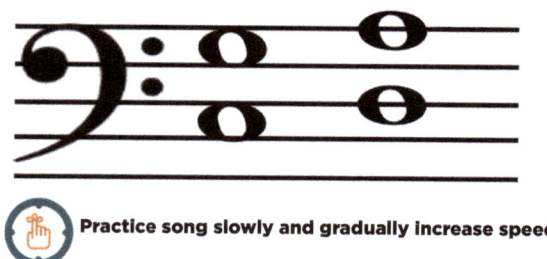

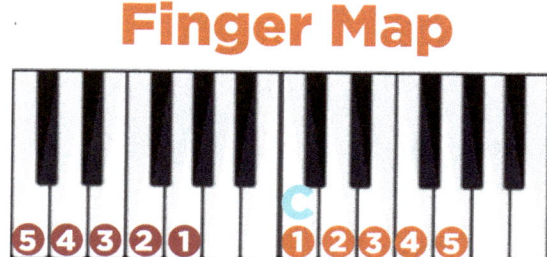

Practice song slowly and gradually increase speed

Finger Map

Mr. Du Bois

Moderately

Thanks Clas –	Mis – sic!	ter Time –	Du less!	Bois Taught	You us

paved
through · the
es – · way!
says!

W.E.B. Du Bois

W.E.B. Du Bois (1868-1963) was born in Great Barrington, Massachusetts. Du Bois was an author, historian, and civil rights activist. Graduating from Harvard University, he was the first African American to earn a doctorate. DuBois was the co-founder of The NAACP. He wrote extensively and was a very popular spokesperson for African American rights during the first half of the 20th century. He is best known for his classic work "The Souls of Black Folk."

Practice!

+ **Name the intervals**

+ **Play the intervals**

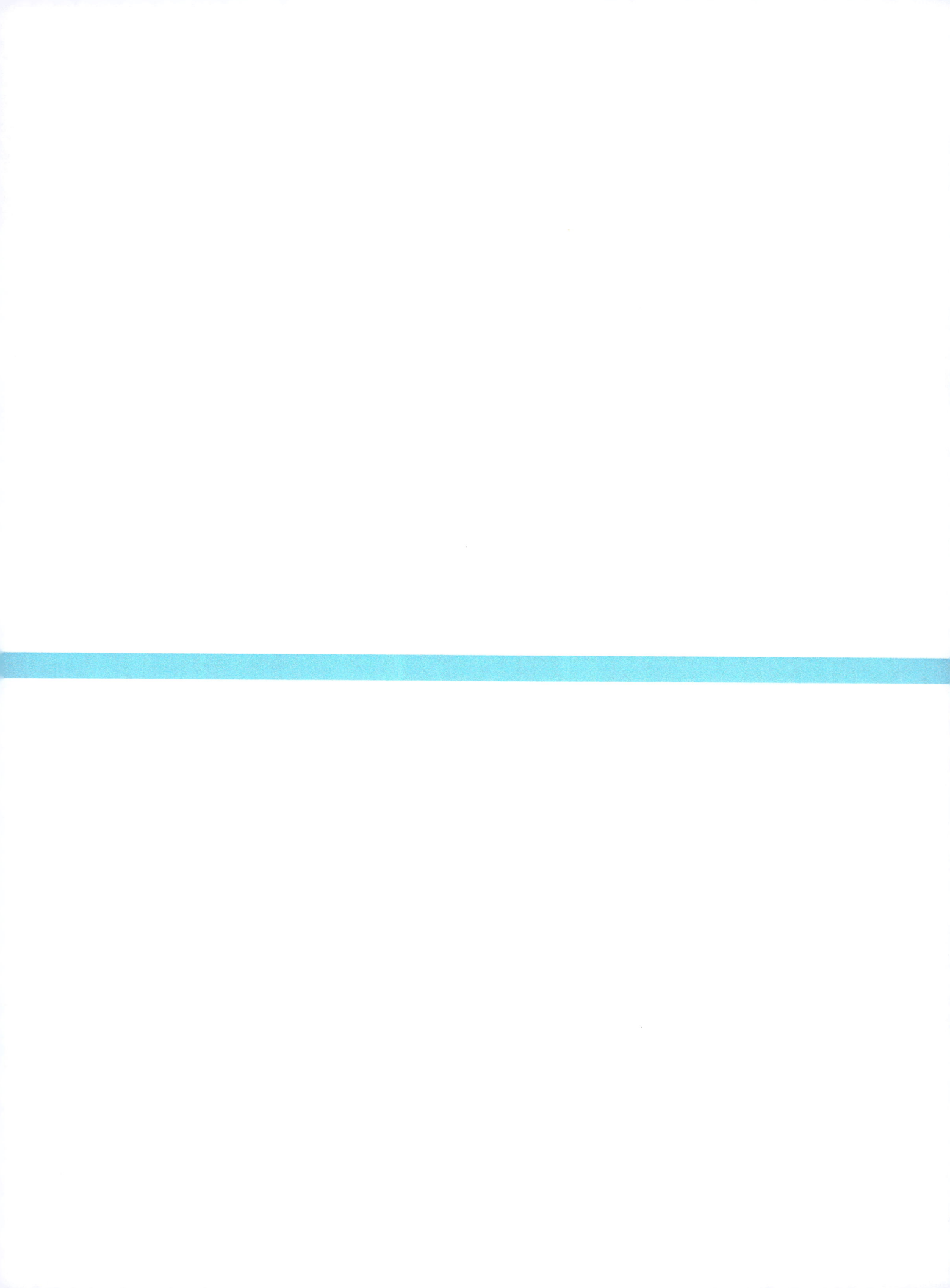

Unit 6

Rests, Accidentals, Ties

Rests

A **REST** is a duration of silence. That means no music is being played.

A **QUARTER REST** is a musical pause that lasts for one beat. In other words, it is one beat of silence.

quarter rest

Practice!

 + **Practice clapping the rhythm**

Don't clap on the rests

Don't forget to repeat!

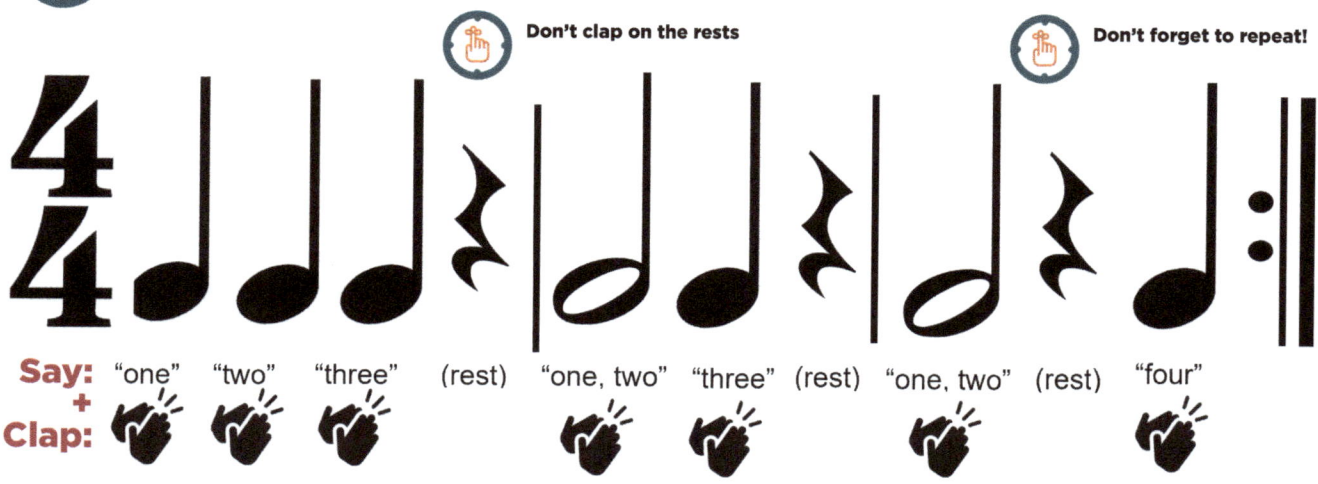

Say: "one" "two" "three" (rest) "one, two" "three" (rest) "one, two" (rest) "four"
+ Clap:

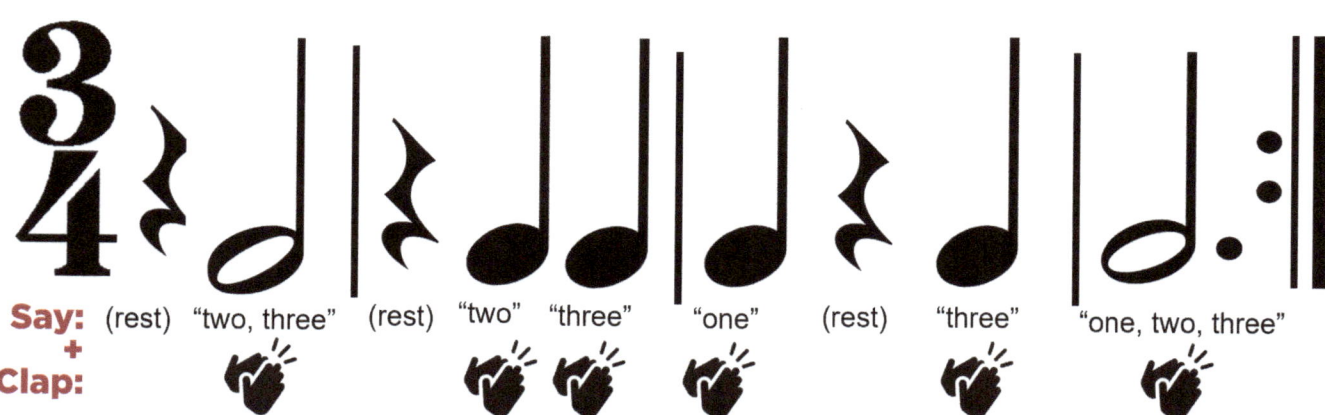

Say: (rest) "two, three" (rest) "two" "three" "one" (rest) "three" "one, two, three"
+ Clap:

+ **How many beats of silence does a quarter rest get?**

+ **How many white keys do you skip to play a fifth?**

+ **Circle the time signature in the song below**

Review Time!

Practice!

+ **Circle all the quarter rests**

+ **Clap the rhythm of the song**

+ **Name the intervals**

Finger Map

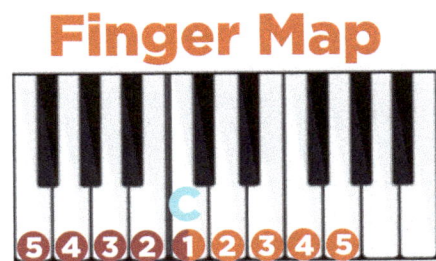

Give it a Rest

Practice!

+ **Circle each quarter rest**

+ **Clap the rhythm of the treble clef**

+ **Name the intervals**

Finger Map

In the Garden

Flowing

f In the gar-den | we play! | Flow-ers and sun

all day! | Worms and slugs and | creep-ing bugs will

put a smile on | your face.

92

Flat

In musical terms, **PITCH** describes how high or low a sound is.

FLAT means lower in pitch. When you see this symbol that means you are to play the key that is a half step lower.

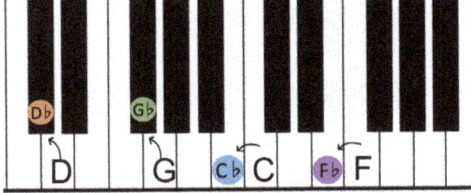

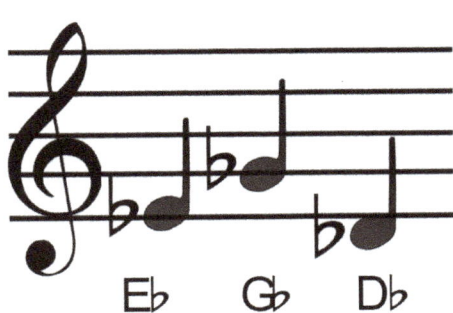

A half step down is the closest key to the left.

 Even white keys can be flat!

On the music staff, a flat sign is placed to the left of the note to signify that the note is flat.

Eb   Gb   Db

Practice!

+ **Name the flat note**

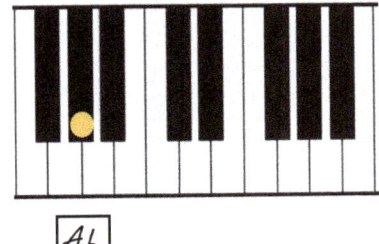

Ab

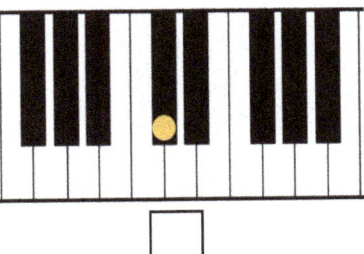

+ **Name the notes**

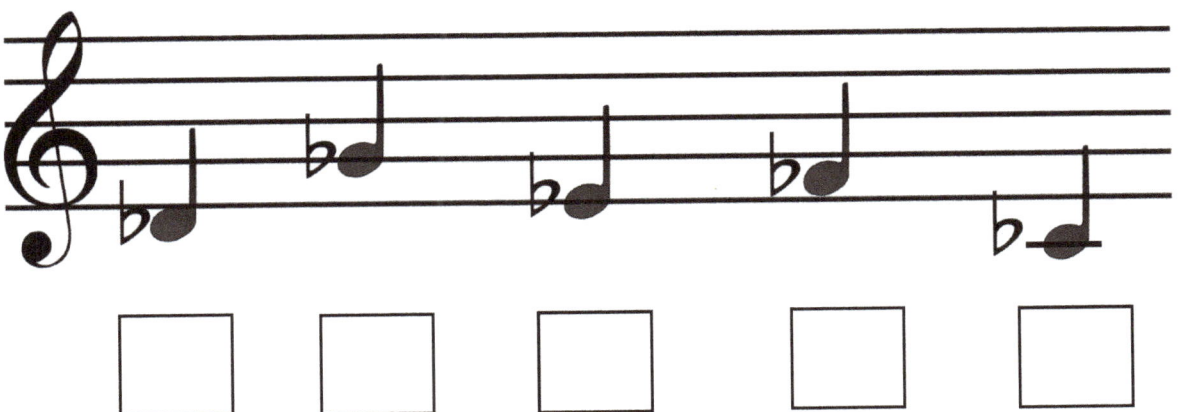

Practice!

+ **Fill in the note names**

Get Creative!
Press the damper pedal
while playing.

Nightfall

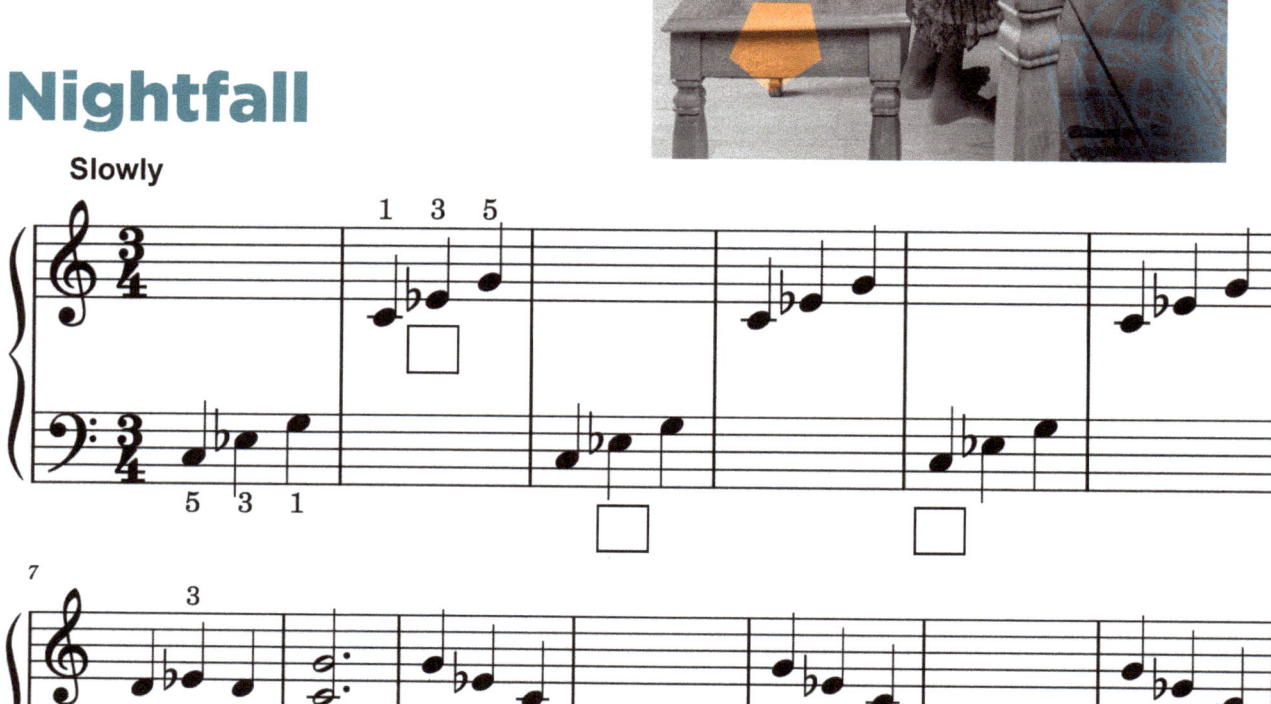

94

Whole Rest

A **WHOLE REST** is a musical pause that lasts for four beats. In other words, it is four beats of silence.

When a note is flat, it remains flat for the whole measure. The flat symbol will not be written again. When you get to a new measure, the note is no longer flat. The flat sign must be written again if it is to be played flat.

Practice!

+ **Circle all the flat notes**

Finger Map

(5) (4) (3) (2) (1) C 1 2 3 4 5

Can I Sleep in Your Room?

A note is flat for an entire measure.

Moderately

Can   I   sleep   in   your   room?   I   heard   a
Can   I   sleep   in   your   room?   Was   too   dark

Whole rest. LH does not play any music

4

thump!   Can   I   sleep   in   you   room?
see!   Can   you   sleep   in   my   room?

7

Did   you   hear   that   loud   bump?
Come   now,   and   sleep   with   me.

Still flat!

95

Sharp

SHARP means higher in pitch. When you see this symbol ♯ that means you are to play the key that is a half step higher.

When a note is sharp, it remains sharp for the whole measure.

When you get to a new measure, the note is no longer sharp. The sharp sign must be written again if it is to be played sharp.

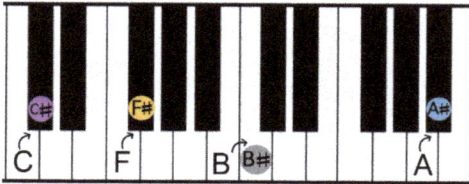

A half step up is the closest key to the right.

White keys can be sharp too!

On the music staff, a sharp sign is placed to the left of the note to signify that the note is sharp.

D♯　G♯　F♯

Practice!

+ **Name the sharp note**

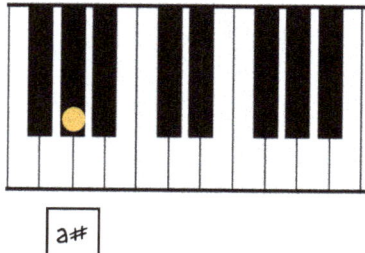

a♯

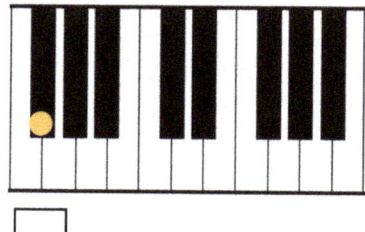

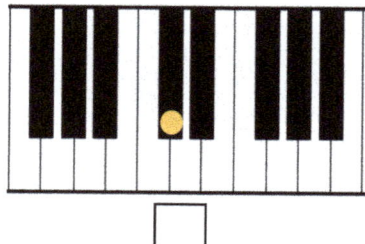

+ **Name the notes**

Notice the first measure of the song. It only has one beat. This is called a **PICK UP MEASURE** or an **INCOMPLETE MEASURE**. This allows songs to start on another beat besides "1." This song starts on beat 3!

Finger Map

A Poet's Tune

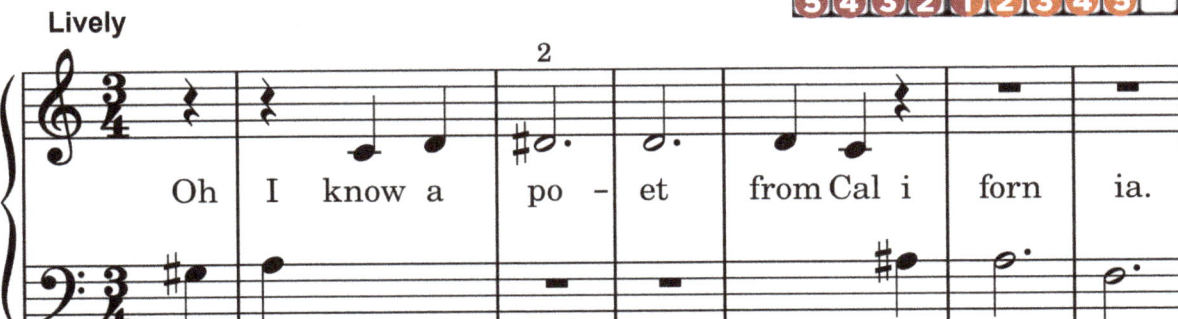

Lively

Oh I know a po - et from Cal i forn ia.

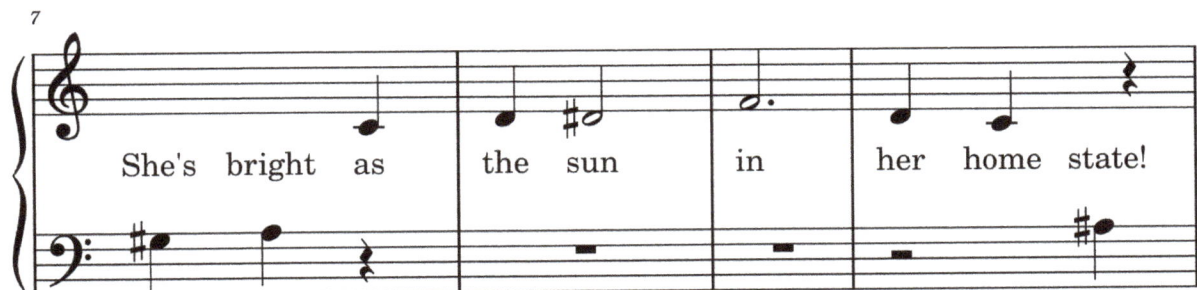

She's bright as the sun in her home state!

A man da Gor man!

Amanda Gorman

Amanda Gorman (1998) was born and raised in Los Angeles, California. She was named the first ever National Youth Poet Laureate of the United States. She is the author of "The Hill We Climb: An Inaugural Poem for the Country. At the age of 22, she read this poem at the 2021 Inauguration, making her the youngest inaugural poet.

Natural Sign

The **NATURAL SIGN** is used to cancel an accidental (previous sharp or flat note). When you see this symbol, you no longer play a sharp or flat note; instead, you play the natural note.

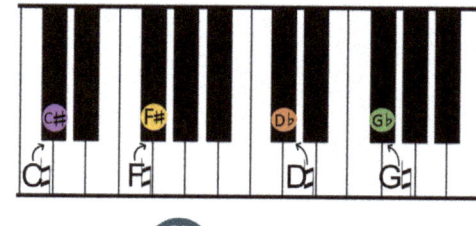

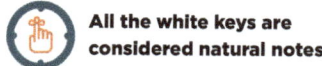

All the white keys are considered natural notes.

On the music staff, a natural sign is placed to the left of the note to signify that the note is no longer sharp or flat in a measure.

Practice!

+ **Fill in note names**

+ **Circle the natural signs**

+ **How many sharp notes are there?**
   Hint: A note remains sharp within the measure unless there's a natural sign.

Secret Treasure

98

Ties

A **TIE** is a curved line connecting two notes that are on the same line or space. It means that you will only play it **ONE TIME** but will hold it for the combined value of the notes.

Press middle C once but hold it for 2 beats.

1 + 1 = 2 beats

2 + 2 = 4 beats

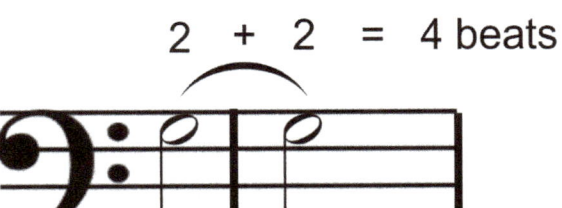

Press G once but hold it for 4 beats.

Practice!

+ **Play the notes and fill in the blanks**   Only play the note once!

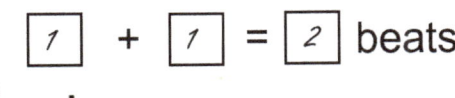

1 + 1 = 2 beats

☐ + ☐ = ☐ beats

☐ + ☐ = ☐ beats

☐ + ☐ = ☐ beats

Practice!

+ **Circle all the ties and clap the rhythm of the song**
Hint, notice the difference between a tie and a slur.

When I Feel Lonely

Slowly

100

Staccato

STACCATO means playing each note short and detached. This is the opposite of legato. To play staccato, quickly lift your fingers off the keys.

When a note is staccato, there will be a small dot above or below the note

Practice!

+ **Circle all the staccato notes**

+ **Trace all the slurs**

Double Dutch

Allegretto: Moderately Fast

Cha - llenge - chall - enge / List - en to the / one! / beat! / Jump - ing rope is / Then you move your / fun! / feet!

Play short and detached

Out side to play / Bounce and to hop and / with friends and such / criss and cross. There

is best with doub - / is so much you / le dutch! / can do!

⚠ *F is no longer sharp!*

Unit 7

G Position

G Position

When we play in **G POSITION** on the treble clef staff, finger 1 in the right hand starts on treble G. Remember, the letters ascend in alphabetical order.

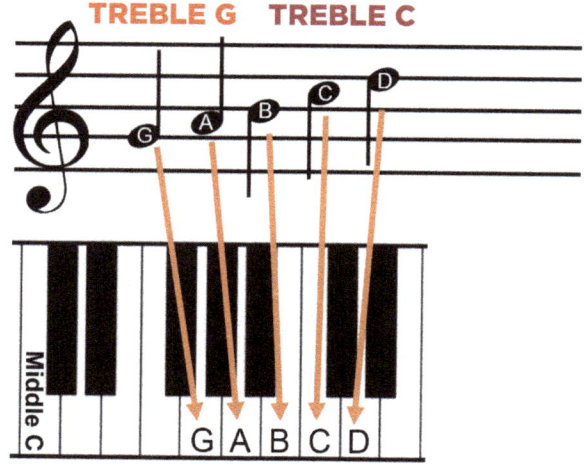

TREBLE G   TREBLE C

The **G MAJOR PENTASCALE** is G, A, B, C, and D.

Practice!

+ **Fill in the note names**

Right Hand G Position

Moderately

Right hand only

104

When we play in G Position on the bass clef staff, finger 5 in the left hand starts on the G below BASS C.

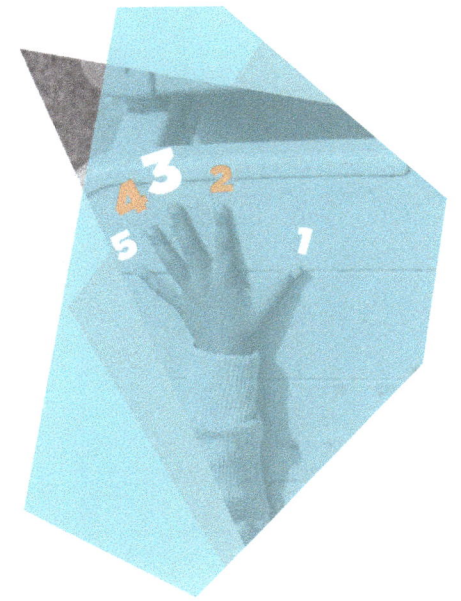

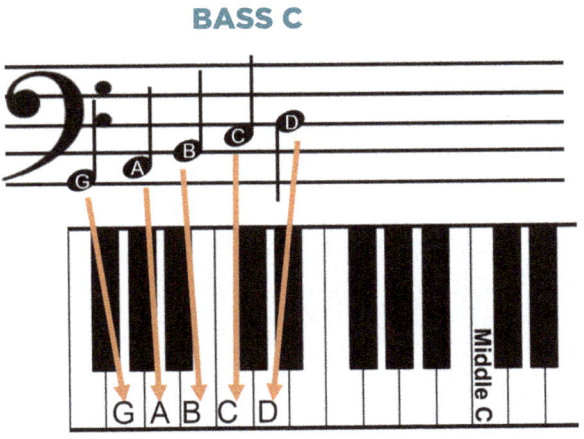

The **G MAJOR PENTASCALE** is G, A, B, C, and D.

Practice!

+ Circle the notes of the G major pentascale

+ Fill in the note names

Left Hand G Position

D.C. al Fine

D. C. AL FINE, short for an Italian phrase, Da Capo al Fine, means repeat from the beginning and play to the end.

Practice!

+ **What is the time signature?**

+ **Clap the rhythm of the notes on the treble clef staff**
  Hint: Watch out for sharp notes!

Grandmother's Mantlepiece

Moderato: Moderate, medium speed

Grand-moth-ers man-tel piece has pict-ures of — fam-ly
Guess he is fam i ly! Right next to my aunt-y his

Hold!!   Fine   *F is still sharp!*

and some of them I have nev-er met. There's one of ma-ma
pic-ture is part of our his tor-y! *Shift hands*

one of O bam a She says he rep re sents what black folks

D.C. al Fine

ov – er came!   *Repeat from the beginning and play to the end (Fine).*

Fine is Italian for **END**

106

Review Time!

+ **What does D.C. al Fine mean?**

+ **What does Fine mean?**

Barack Obama

Barack Obama (1961) was born in Honolulu, Hawaii. He was the 44th president of The United States of America. Obama was the first African American to become president. He served two terms: 2008 and 2012.

The Fight

Andante: moderately slow, walking pace

Octaves

An **OCTAVE** is played when you skip 6 white keys. It can be played as a melodic interval or a harmonic interval.

On a music staff an octave is written as a **SPACE NOTE** going to a **LINE NOTE** OR a **LINE NOTE** going to a **SPACE NOTE**.

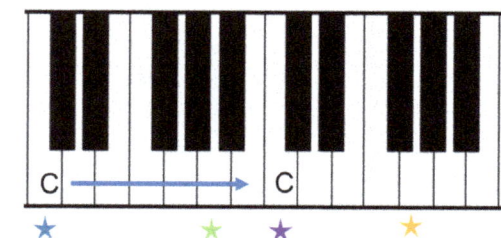

Playing a bass C and then playing middle C is going up → an octave. When you play any octave, you will always land on a key with the same letter name.

Space to Line

Up an octave

Line to Space

Down an octave

Simone Biles

Simone Biles (1997) was born in Columbus, Ohio. She is the most decorated American Gymnast with more than two dozen Olympic and World Championship medals to her name. Biles is the first woman ever to perform a Yurchenko Double Pike in competition. This move is so challenging and dangerous that many suspect no other woman will even train to try it! Biles also has several distinctive and difficult gymnastic moves named after her.

Fermata

A **FERMATA** is a symbol that tells you to hold a note longer than its normal value. Fermatas are great for dramatic pauses and endings.

Practice!

+ **Review each term and find it in the song**

  + Legato
  + Staccato
  + Fermata
  + Quarter rest
  + Octave

The Grand Finale

Vivace: Fast

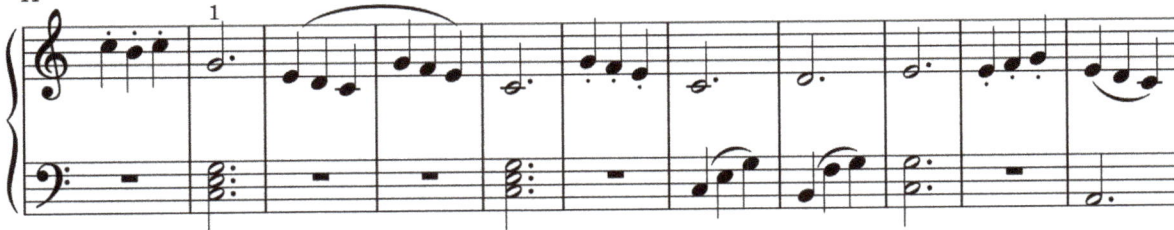

 **Practice one hand at a time. Start slow and gradually increase tempo of the song. Hands shift throughout the song.**

109

Lift Every Voice and Sing

Moderato: Moderate, medium speed

James Weldon Johnson

James Weldon Johnson (1871-1938) was born in Jacksonville, Florida. He was an American writer, composer and civil rights activist. He was also a distinguished lawyer and served as Executive Secretary in the NAACP. Johnson wrote the lyrics for the Black National Anthem, Lift Every Voice and Sing.

J. Rosamond Johnson

J. Rosamond Johnson (1873-1954) was born in Jacksonville, Florida. He was a pianist, songwriter, producer, soldier, singer and actor. Johnson partnered with his older brother James Weldon Johnson and composed Lift Every Voice and Sing. Around 1900, when he composed the song, he taught it to children all around Jacksonville, Florida. It became so popular that it became known as the Black National Anthem.

Notes

Notes

Blank Staff Paper